POUPONNE AND BALTHAZAR

POUPONNE AND BALTHAZAR

by

Sidonie de la Houssaye

translated, with an introduction by

J. John Perret

Published by
The Center for Louisiana Studies
University of Southwestern Louisiana

Library of Congress Catalog Number: 83-72072
ISBN Number: 0-940984-16-4

Published by The Center for Louisiana Studies
University of Southwestern Louisiana

[Author's dedication]

To my grandchildren

[Translator's dedication]

To Mary

CONTENTS

ACKNOWLEDGEMENTS

Two colleagues offered invaluable assistance in the preparation of this translation. Professor Viron L. Barnhill is a specialist in linguistics and contemporary American English usage. He grew up in Southwest Louisiana in a bilingual household next-door to a grandmother who spoke only Acadian French. Professor George F. Reinecke grew up in a bilingual family in New Orleans. A medievalist, he is also interested in the language, traditions, and culture of southern Louisiana. He has directed many theses in these areas and is a recognized authority in dialectology.

The translator, however, takes full responsiblity for any errors.

My wife Mary offered valuable suggestions and proofread with me.

INTRODUCTION

Sidonie de la Houssaye was already forty-seven when in 1867 we first hear of her as a writer,[1] and had reached sixty-eight when her first original long fiction was published. She continued writing until late 1892, less than eighteen months before her death at the age of seventy-four. There are dated manuscripts going back to 1880, but they are unpublished stories written for her grandchildren's edification. Her first authenticated original fiction belongs to 1885, and there was a period of some seven years during which she exerted herself to the extent of producing eight novels and novellas. Her previous work consisted in large measure of translation and, as we shall see, of literary assistance to George Washington Cable. In 1888, or in about the middle of her most active period, she published *Pouponne and Balthazar*. That same year her fellow Louisianian, George Dessommes, published *Tante Cydette*, the story of a Creole maiden aunt whose opportunistic and amoral approach to matchmaking and strength of will suggest a heroine cast in the mold of Balzac's Cousine Bette. Her work, on the other hand, is directly attributable to Cable's suggestion in 1887 that she write an Acadian romance. He offered this advice during the course of his only visit to her home in Franklin.[2]

Though she, like George Dessommes, was a Louisiana Creole, she was widely separated from him by age, sex, rural upbringing, limited education, and inexperience--she never left her native state. Yet there are striking features which they had in common. First, both, having known and lost relative affluence, expected some financial return from their work. She entertained the greater expectations and did earn some royalties, but she fell far short of the security she so vigorously pursued. Second, they both used the French language as their medium, though fully cognizant that it could command but a small audience. Third, they were both willing to attempt "daring" subjects and follow new and suspect trends in literature: thus both took much notice of Zola with her tendencies in this regard being more evident in the novels that antedate

1. *L'Epoque* [New Orleans], December 22, 1867.

2. Sidonie de la Houssaye. Letter to George Washington Cable, August 17, 1887. William Beer Cable Collection, Howard Tilton Memorial Library, Tulane University. All letters, unless otherwise designated are from this collection and used with permission.

Pouponne.

The daughter of Ursin Perret and Françoise Pain, Hélène Perret was born August 17, 1820, in the civil parish of St. John the Baptist about thirty-five miles upriver from New Orleans. The writer-to-be was always known as Sidonie, although this name is not on her baptismal certificate, which is still preserved in the church at Edgard. Her father moved his growing family in 1828 to St. Mary Parish, west of the Atchafalaya and southwest of New Orleans. There he became a successful sugar planter and the owner of Belle Vue Plantation in the Irish Bend section of Bayou Teche above the town of Franklin. According to the highly romanticized autobiographical sketch, "Une Page de ma vie," which is only fragmentarily available, his daughter received her education from a governess. As for institutional education, she spent less than three months at the new Sacred Heart Convent in St. James Parish on the Mississippi. There she was enrolled in the second or highest class, the normal curriculum of which included, besides religious subjects, the history of the Ancients, of France, and modern chronology, arithmetic and geometry, as well as vocabulary and (French) literary style. One may gauge the depth of this last study from the fact that the only book mentioned is the *Fables* of the nineteenth century Jesuit educator Loriquet. After the convent school closed in May, 1833, because of a cholera epidemic, she never returned. Her stay was less than three months; she was twelve years old at the time.[3] It was common for well-to-do- plantation girls to go to a convent to prepare for the reception of First Communion and Confirmation, and twelve was the normal age for these ceremonies.

Ursin Perret's library is to a considerable degree still extant in Jeanerette. How much use she made of its contents is not known, but it could have afforded her access to the French, English, and Latin classics. In several works she lists "the great authors" but rarely indicates anything more than a nodding acquaintance with them. Thus, though expressing a great admiration for Lamartine, the one poem she cites is attributed to the wrong collection. Among other favorite "greats" were Charles Millevoye and Hégésippe Moreau, both largerly forgotten romantics, and Anaïs de Ségalas (1814-95) whose name does not even appear in the standard histories of French literature. Without laboring the point, one can say that her most admired authors have not stood the test of time, with one exception.

3. Letter received from Mother Louise Callan, R.S.C.J., July 25, 1965.

This exception is Alexandre Dumas *père*. Though his literary merit may be questioned, he is certainly not ephemeral. She seemed almost addicted to his romantic view, no longer *à la mode*, except perhaps in French Louisiana. Nearly every hero in her work displays traits of Dumas' *Antony* (1831), in which an impetuous lover, a natural child and pariah, braves society's conventions in an adulterous relationship. He belongs to the literary company of despised poets like Vigny's *Chatterton* and nobles masking as outlaws like Hugo's *Hernani.* Antony, it will be remembered, kills his mistress with her consent and assures her husband that he did it because she resisted him, his purpose being to preserve her "honor."

Mme de la Houssaye's future husband, than a steamboat captain, is depicted much like Dumas' alienated hero in the pseudo-autobiographical "Une Page de ma vie":

> . . . everything pointed to a man accustomed to giving orders. His brown eyes flashed like lightning and one sensed in him a soul with violent passions; and indeed, everything was impetuous and intense in that soul. The captain could do nothing halfway; love, ambition and friendship itself were not just feelings with him.[4]

Outcasts like Antony are the subject of her most extensive and ambitious work, *Les Quarteronnes de la Nouvelle-Orléans*, of which only the first two appeared in book form.[5] Published under the pseudonym of Louise Raymond, this series focuses on the class of young, largely white, "women of color" who were brought up to be "placed" in concubinage with a Caucasian lover. Of course, such women played no part in the social life of the French Caucasian women and families of New Orleans, and were hardly more acceptable among the blacks.

Mme de la Houssaye started her quadroon series in 1885, and borrowed from the elder Dumas. Written in French, these works were to be translated for the American market. As in the supposedly true stories she had earlier sold to Cable for inclusion in *Strange True Stories of Louisiana*, she claimed

4. Velma Savoie, "The Life and Writing of Sidonie de la Houssaye," (MA thesis, Louisiana State University 1936), p. 43.

5. The four novels are: (1) *Octavia la Quarteronne* (1894), (2) *Violetta la Quarteronne* (1895), (3) *Gina la Quarteronne* (1895-97), (4) *Dahlia la Quarteronne* (1897-98).

to have founded this work on manuscripts belonging to her grandmother and entitled "Les Quarteronnes de La Nouvelle-Orléans de 1800 à 1830," though the reputed author in fact had died in 1828. Once Cable wrote her asking if her grandmother was still living in 1836, and she expressed indignation at this questioning of her integrity, leaving the question unanswered. But since the grandmother's manuscripts are a transparent fiction, how much does the work owe to Dumas? We can only presume that the orgies, incest, and stylized scenes of debauchery were inspired by *La Tour de Nesle*, one of the favorite plays of the century, since her own life-experience could hardly have been of any help whatsoever. When, in *Octavia*, a quadroon mistress demands of her lover the famous necklace intended by Cardinal de Rohan for Marie-Antoinette,[6] this can only be the result of the author's memories of Dumas' *Le Collier de la reine* being so vivid that she did not worry about such trivial problems as the reconstitution of the ornament which historically had been sold off piecemeal.

The ending of *Octavia* is also reminiscent of *Antony*: the spurned quadroon, having kidnapped her lover's legitimate daughter and debauched her, takes her final vengeance in having the girl carry on an incestuous relationship with her unrecognized brother, finally arranging to have the father catch his children *flagrante delicto* and kill his daughter, as Antony killed his mistress to preserve the appearance of honor.

From Dumas *fils'* favorite *La Dame aux camélias* she took Marguerite's dislike of scented flowers and transferred it to Octavia. She also used the name Violetta, which is Marguerite's name in the operatic version of the play (*La Traviata*) and used it for the title character of the second novel in the series.

In *Gina* there is a costume ball too close to the characters and settings of Dumas *père's Henri III et sa cour* to be accidental. Among the characters present are replicas of Catherine de Médicis and Ruggièri, the official court astrologer. But in addition there is a sinister masked figure who seems modeled more closely on the aging Don Ruy Gomez de Silva in Hugo's *Hernani* than on any creation of Dumas *père*.

As he reads the series, the reader cannot help thinking of naturalistic hero-

6. Fallen from the favor of Marie-Antoinette, Cardinal de Rohan was led to believe she wanted a necklace valued at 1,500,000 *francs*. He gave it to a swindler impersonating the queen; he was disgraced and the swindlers severely punished.

ines such as Zola's *Nana*. Zola, incidentally, is the only post-romantic writer referred to in her correspondence. In a late letter to Cable she expressed her confusion about Anglo-Saxon morality. It was incomprehensible that the publishers, Messrs. Laird and Lee, should reject *Octavia* when "they do not blush to translate the indecencies of Emile Zola . . . ."[7] But in a curious turnabout three years later she wrote to Zola for help in finding a publisher in France, and received a polite, but impractical, encouragement from the great man.[8] Yet the author did not envision her quadroon heroines as naturalistic types. She envisioned them as romantics, falling back on *fatalité* rather than on naturalistic theory. She ends the last of the series, *Dahlia*, with the statement that these unfortunate women are "Pushed by fate on to the path of evil, and more worthy of pity than scorn." What could she have been thinking of but the romantic Cable's ending to "Madame Delphine," another work concerned with the problems of color: "Lord, lay not this sin to her charge!"

We have seen that Sidonie was engaged to a steamboat captain. Just after her thirteenth birthday she married Pelletier de la Houssaye. Such an early age for marriage was not unknown in nineteenth-century Louisiana; her own mother had married at the same age. Though neither her husband nor her sons habitually used the aristocratic particule before their names, she generally did so. On her wedding day Tinker says she was playing with dolls,[9] but Velma Savoie believes her to have been worldly-wise for her age and associated with a group of girls whose *vade mecum* was a booklet called *The Catechism of a Flirt*.[10] Her school records give her age as sixteen. If this age is wrong, and it assuredly is, as it disagrees with all other documents, it at least testifies to a physical maturity in the soon-to-be-married young woman.

Between 1836 and 1845, the union produced six children, of whom two elder sons, one daughter and a last-born son, survived. The family moved from St. Martinville to Franklin in 1841, when Governor A. B. Roman appoint-

7. Sidonie de la Houssaye, Letter to Cable, November 9, 1889.

8. V. catalog of Swann Auction Sale 448 (November 29, 1956).

9. Edward Larocque Tinker, *Les Ecrits de langue française en Louisiane au XIXe siècle* (Paris, 1932), p. 34.

10. Savoie, "Life and Writing," p. 35.

ed de la Houssaye to a four-year term as sheriff of St. Mary Parish. Unsuccessful in an attempt to be elected, he returned to steamboating. From that time, the financial problems of his wife began. On more than one occasion she took her husband to court to protect her paraphernal rights. In the late 1840's she opened a girls' school which continued until forced to close during the Civil War. In the 1850 census, her husband has no listed occupation. Though 1859 was a sad year in which they were obliged to sell their house to meet outstanding debts, it was brightened a little by the marriage of their daughter Lilia to John Tarlton.

Both her elder son and son-in-law served during the Civil War, but her husband's death, though closely associated in time with the military action in the Irish Bend section of Bayou Teche in April 1863, had nothing to do with the war. The legend that her husband was sheriff and shot down in the line of duty is just that.[11] He had not held office since 1845.

Immediately after the war the widow served as postmistress in Franklin for a brief time and then re-opened her school. She probably continued to teach full-time at least until 1874, at which time she said she began to give serious attention to writing. In 1875 her daughter died, leaving behind her eight children and an unemployed son-in-law. John Tarlton was then thirty-seven, handsome and in good health; why he left the care and sustenance of his children to their grandmother remains unclear. However, Mme de la Houssaye always referred to herself as their sole support. She accepted the burden willingly in an almost unhealthy display of "smother love." Seeming to have been worried about the possibility of her son-in-law's remarriage, she deeded her house to her grandchildren on the sole condition that she always have a room there, even though she realized that in so doing she could never use it as a boarding house or source of revenue.

Though the 1870's were largely devoted to bringing up the Tarlton brood, she was trying to write. Her father died in 1877. She returned to teaching in 1882, but by January 1884 she was in desperate need of work. Her first major authenticated literary endeavor, a translation of *Sybille* by the popular novelist May Agnes Fleming, came out as a serial under the title of *Le Mari de Marguerite* in the latter part of 1883 in *L'Abeille*, the leading French newspaper in New Orleans.

Her notions of publishing practices and literary ethics run the gamut from

11. Tinker, *Les Ecrits*, p. 108

the naive to the devious. Thus, in 1883 she had offered *L'Abeille* the French text of a manuscript and simultaneously sent the *Times-Democrat*, another New Orleans daily, and English translation, quite unconcerned about their running simultaneously in rival publications. This was "Voyage de ma grand-mère," the reputed record of her grandmother's trip from New Orleans via flatboat to St. Martinville in the 1790's. Later this literary fraud was to have embarrassing consequences for George Washington Cable, who bought it through an agent for inclusion in his *Strange True Stories of Louisiana*. From January 1884 to January 1890, she and Cable carried on a correspondence as entertaining as it is informative about both of them, though no Cable scholar has yet taken proper advantage of it. Regrettably, only her letters to him are preserved. In these her theme never varies: I need work; I need money; I will translate; I will teach for you in New England; use my materials and put your name on them (presumably justified by Dumas *pere's* employment of a stable of ghost-writers). When I interviewed them some years ago, elderly people whose parents she knew and others who had received at least part of their education from Mme de la Houssaye retained from youth an image of Cable as a rotten pseudo-Southerner who had shamelessly plundered her materials and published them in his own name. But there is no truth in this view. Whatever borrowing took place is hers, not his. The correspondence in summary is a series of exchanges between a man seeking historical facts and hard evidence and a woman equally determined to use every evasive and dilatory tactic to suggest that proof for her alleged facts was just around the corner, or had just burned up in a courthouse or church fire, or had just become unavailable because of the death of a centenarian eyewitness. The established writer tolerated her jeremiads and constant pleas for help, and even put up with her patently manufactured information, all because he needed her. Ever since the publication of "Tite Poulette" and "Jean-ah Poquelin" in the October 1847 and May 1875 issues of *Scribner's Monthly*, his dialectal inaccuracies--and therefore his reliability, were in some doubt, because of an article which challenged them in the *Boston Literary World*. In reply to the editor of the *World*, Cable went so far as to present himself as a Creole.[12] Perhaps he could justify the term in that it once meant "native-born" and nothing more, but it was clearly a disingenuous equivocation, if not a bold-faced lie. Cable was neither a member

12. Philip Butcher, *George W. Cable* (New York: Twayne Publishers, Inc., 1962), p. 44.

of the French-speaking population, nor was he at all popular with its members once his stories began to appear. As she hoped he would be her key to financial success, he needed her because he needed a Creole to testify publicly to the American reader that "he is one of us," in spite of the historian Gayarre's offer to review a Cable book if the novelist could name two respectable Creole families where he was welcome to visit--a challenge Cable did not take up.[13] In her he found a *bona fide* Creole begging for a chance to provide the author of *Old Creole Days* with raw materials for further local color. She was middle-aged, presumably naive, living in a sleepy town at some distance from the opinions and prejudices of the metropolis; she seemed ready to make any sacrifice to support her family. She could serve both as a Creole friend and as an authority to whom he could allude to by name in the preface to his forthcoming *Strange True Stories*. She was also a ready-made scapegoat for such errors and anachronisms as might have escaped him in the manuscripts she had sold to him. When in fact he did so use her in an embarrassing apology published in *Century Magazine*,[14] he doubtelessly accelerated the breaking off of their correspondence. Perhaps he had no further need for her, since his artistic attentions were chiefly now directed away from French Louisiana.

If she had been asked to evaluate her relationship with Cable, she would have had to answer that it brought her more notoriety than fame and fortune, but her literary reputation was certainly enhanced by his previously mentioned visit to Franklin in 1887. His own Acadian story, *Bonaventure*, was soon to appear. He recommended that she try her hand at an Acadian romance. She turned almost inescapably to the great theme long since determined by Longfellow, the separation of lovers at the time of the expulsion from Nova Scotia, but invested with local color and provided with a happy ending.

This attempt is an obvious reaction to the misfortunes of the quadroon series and of *Claire* which still remains unpublished although she described it to Cable as "my pet work."[15] She had sent this work along with *Octavia* to Charles Scribner in 1885. Some time before she met Cable she had offered

13. Charles Gayarré, "Mr. Cable's Freedman's Case in Equity," *Times-Democrat* [New Orleans], January 11, 1885.

14. George W. Cable, Letter, *Century Magazine*, XXXVIII (September, 1889), 798-99.

15. Sidonie de la Houssaye, Letter to Cable, September 12, 1885.

to send the firm some Louisiana sketches, and on being asked to send some specimens had instead set to work on the quadroon romances, which were only published locally and very late, the last three in fact being posthumous publications. All were under the pseudonym of Louise Raymond. *Claire* is a kind of romantic version of the Goncourts' early naturalistic drama *Henriette Maréchale* which failed in its 1865 Paris première. It is a tale of a girl's sacrificial marriage to her mother's lover so as to save both mother and lover from death at the hands of the suspicious father. Without love the heroine pines away and dies within a few months of the marriage, whereupon her own true lover follows her within a few days, and they are buried together like Tristan and Iseult by the repentant husband.

Of a similar soap-opera scandalous type was *Frère et Soeur* (Brother and Sister). It is also supposedly based on facts observed by the author. As the title is suggestive enough of the contents, we may condense the 425-page manuscript by saying that it contains, besides incest, attempted abortion followed by infanticide, parricide, suicide, and assorted accidental deaths. Since we know that Cable warned Charlès Scribner not to touch *Claire* or *Octavia*, heaven knows what he or the equally puritanical publisher would have said of this last-discussed work.

Various noble and altruistic motives have been attributed to her quadroon novels, of which *Octavia* was the first. Auguste Viatte, the Swiss critic, grouped them with Alfred Mercier's *L'Habitation Saint-Ybars* (1881) and Charles Testut's *Le Vieux Salomon* (1858, pub. 1872) as a protest against color prejudice.[16] But the prosaic truth is that she was trying to capitalize on a risqué topic of current interest. Perhaps she mistook this aspect of the works of Zola and the naturalists for the element which conferred true literary merit upon that French school. Surely she achieved frank treatment of the seamier side of life far more than she mastered naturalistic method. Had she studied in France, she would have realized that the French give equal, if not greater weight to *forme* (style) than to *fond* (content).

Once these works had been rejected, she obviously reacted and adopted a more "proper" vein, not only in *Pouponne and Balthazar*, but also in *Charles et Ella*, and *Amis et Fortune* (Friends and Fortune), which followed in 1891 and 1892. The first is brief, and tells of a poor boy in remote Louisiana who

16. Auguste Viatte, *Historie littéraire de l'Amérique française: des origines à 1950* (Paris, 1954), p. 295.

falls in love with a girl far above his station. The dilemma is shamelessly resolved by making Charles' father the ill-treated nephew of a Scottish lord. Disappearing for seven years, he returns with money, manners and a title and the wedding is celebrated almost immediately.

Amis et Fortune, almost ten times as long as *Charles et Ella*, was serialized in 1892 in *Le Meschacébé* located in Reserve, Louisiana. A wealthy but crippled heiress switches roles with her servant to fathom the intentions of her suitors somewhat in the manner of a play by Marivaux. Her device is effective, and she eventually finds happiness. In neither work is originality much sought after. They are potboilers pure and simple.

Her last work, *Dahlia*, completed the quadroon series. Raised in a Baltimore convent school, the heroine only learns in her teens what her background is and the impossible situation confronting her. Unlike Honoré Grandissime, f.m.c., in Cable's novel who had a similar background and committed suicide, she "adjusted" to the situation.

The obsession with money which this last work betrays borders on the pathological. Here are four phrases almost randomly selected from the work.

> "By paying, one obtains everything."
> "Money is a powerful ally."
> "Money makes the laws everywhere."
> "With money we overcome all obstacles."

Perhaps it was the fact that her polite fiction was hardly more successful than her racier novels that led her back to the attitudes of *Dahlia*, but perhaps, too, it is Sidonie herself who was the Zola character, dominated by the socio-economic forces of her time and frustration. At any rate it seems pointless to suggest any psychologic split between Louise Raymond and Sidonie de la Houssaye.

In 1890 she won *ex aequo* the gold medal of *lauréate* of the *Athénée Louisianais*, a literary society founded in New Orleans in 1876 to preserve the French language in Louisiana. Neither of her two entries, "La Fauvette et le poète," an allegory, and "L'Amour qui renferme en lui seul tous les amours," a prose pastoral, bears any close resemblance to her known style, and one may entertain serious doubts that she really wrote them at all. If so, there is an irony beyond words in the picture of the stately, stiff old woman silently walking up to receive her medal in the full knowledge that though the public had afforded her no acclaim for her extensive and original works she was being crowned by her provincial world's most notable literary group for someone else's endeavor.[17] A desire to humiliate her critics privately in her own mind was a probable motivation for such a performance. An even stronger motivation could have been the cash prize accompanying the gold medal. Less than four years later, she died after a long illness on February 18, 1894.

Sidonie de la Houssaye: The Writer

Allusion has been made to her fascination with and extensive borrowing from Dumas *père*. Stylistically, save for the novel under consideration, she never attempted to emulate his almost excessive use of local color. Untrained in the visual arts, she was not like George Dessommes, who would fit Théophile Gautier's description of himself: "a man for whom the visible world exists." Her Creole contemporary set his scene with the same meticulous attention to detail that Balzac had used in describing the Pension Vauquer at the beginning of *Père Goriot*. By contrast, physical description played a relatively small part in her work. Her palette was rudimentary. She used a Stendahlian approach in which the attempt is to seize the characteristic gesture, psychological trait or phrase that epitomizes the character. We get to know a personality more than a catalog of physical attributes. Abstract nouns, not adjectives, create the portrait.

Her method is not without inherent dangers. Characters sometimes adhere too rigidly to the mold in which they are cast, and the possibility exists that they may become types or monomaniacs as in Balzac and Molière, or even "temperaments" as the deterministic Zola would say. Static characters and a simplistic psychology are often concomitant problems for practitioners of this school. She was aware of these pitfalls and the development in the writer's craft is marked from the first to the last of the quadroon series. *Octavia*, the first, is hatred and vengeance incarnate. By the time she reached *Dahlia*, the last, she has explored the psychology and motivation of these victims of fate and portrays them in a multidimensional manner.

In her insistence on using "historical" or "true" stories, she also differed markedly from Dessommes. With the exception of a mythology written for

17. Alfred Mercier, Diary excerpts, 1890, pp. 97-99. Rudolph Matas Papers. School of Medicine Library, Tulane University.

her grandchildren, it is hard to recall a single novel or story that was not based on history or personally observed events. She introduced her Bossier ancestors in "Voyage de ma grand-mère." "The Young Aunt with the White Hair" (in *Strange True Stories of Louisiana*), and in several unpublished works. Her insistence on the historicity of her narratives must be taken with the proverbial grain of salt. Pierre Bossier, her great-grandfather, is French Flemish in *Pouponne and Balthazar*. He is Alsatian in "The Young Aunt with the White Hair."[18] In "Voyage de ma grand-mere" he is a Prussian![19]

Pouponne and Balthazar

Comparisons with Longfellow's *Evangeline*, the archetypal Acadian heroine, are not rewarding. Aside from the fact that both narrate stories of betrothed couples separated by exile, they have few other parallels. Longfellow's poem ends in a brief reunion before death. Gabriel Lajeunesse literally died in the arms of his beloved Evangeline Bellefontaine, who had already died to the world by assuming the veil of a religious. *Pouponne and Balthazar*, on the other hand, ends on a note of optimism after the couple's marriage. The poet, who like Chateaubriand, described Louisiana without having seen it, created a pastoral atmosphere that evokes Acadiana and its inhabitants with as little accuracy as did the beribboned sheep of a seventeenth-century pastoral depict the daily life of the peasants and their smelly charges.

A more probable, though not certain, influence was Bernardin de Saint-Pierre's *Paul et Virginie* (1787). Even though the setting of the latter is the exotic island of Mauritius in the Indian Ocean, one can find several parallels between the eponymous heroes and heroines of both works. In each case the couples grow up in bucolic settings. From their earliest days they share the joys of childhood and inevitably fall in love. Fatherless, as was Pouponne, and enticed by promises of an inheritance, Virginie goes to live and study with an aunt in mainland France. She blossoms intellectually, but the restrictions of civilization are too much for this child of nature. She must return to Mauritius and to Paul, who had learned to read and write to correspond

18. George W. Cable, *Strange True Stories of Louisiana* (New York, 1889), p. 26.

19. *Ibid.*, p. 110.

with her. Pouponne's education and Balthazar's foundation in the rudiments come to mind. Virginie rejected her inheritance and started homeward, only to drown in view of Paul as her ship ran upon rocks, Paul's efforts to reach it having failed. He died a few weeks later, the victim of a broken heart.

Philosophically, the narratives are poles apart. Bernardin de Saint-Pierre was a disciple of Rousseau. His couple exemplified the joys and natural goodness of man in a primitive state. They symbolizied the perfection of natural religion. Virginie died because she foolishly attempted to reconcile her values with those of a corrupted civilization. *Pouponne and Balthazar*, on the other hand, shows a couple growing up naturally while following the precepts of the Roman Catholic Church. Père Jacques' presence is all-pervasive; he is as much a temporal as a spiritual leader. There is no question of the inherent goodness of man. Man's fallen nature shows--even at wedding receptions.

From the point of realistic portrayal, or as an example of the *roman de moeurs* (novel of manners), how does Mme de la Houssaye's work rate? Within this limited context she does well indeed. The reader is introduced into a well-defined culture that is faithfully represented in all its facets. We know the mores, the traditions, the values, and even the hard-to-define virtues of a unique group. The Acadian philosophy and *joie de vivre* is indelibly impressed on the reader by the exact, though disapproving, description of the Acadian wedding feast. Acadian honesty, industry, thrift, and devotion to God and country run through the composition like motifs, though she felt compelled to apologize to her Creole audience for speaking well of the exiles.

Even in her old age, Sidonie de la Houssaye shared with her younger contemporary Professor Alcée Fortier of Tulane University a snobbish and condescending attitude vis-à-vis the Acadians. After a visit to an Acadian family living next door to her grandson, she observed: ". . . they live in the middle of civilization and don't want to be civilized."[20] In his *Louisiana Studies* Professor Fortier notes: "The greatest default of the Acadian is the little interest they take in education; a great many are completely illiterate."[21]

Stylistically, the author cannot be faulted for the simple, almost primitive tone adopted in this work. *Here* it is appropriate. Images are few and limited

20. Sidonie de la Houssaye, Letter to Cable, June 26, 1887.

21. Alcee Fortier, *Louisiana Studies* (New Orleans, 1894), p. 175.

to similes of almost Homeric simplicity. There are weaknesses to be sure: the repetition of phrases such as "Let it be noted" or "Let us say at once" is one that comes to mind.

Her real strength was in dialogue involving dialectal or regional speech. Her use of *créole*, the patois of the uneducated Negroes, is superbly demonstrated in both prose and song in *Les Quarteronnes de la Nouvelle-Orléans*. If she had a peer in this patois, it could only have been the author of *L'Habitation Saint-Ybars*, Dr. Alfred Mercier. No one could rival her in the reproduction of Acadian French. It is there with all its color, vigor, archaisms and unique pronunciation. How refreshing it is to see its authentic flavor captured now that there is a plethora of unskilled entertainers calling themselves "Cajun raconteurs."

Is there more than a simple, pathetic narrative in *Pouponne and Balthazar*? Mme de la Houssaye would have been surprised to learn that there is. The didacticism is purely involuntary and appears to have escaped the author herself. This very fact makes it more palatable and quite compatible with the simplicity and *naïveté* that permeate every aspect of its composition.

Whereas she would make Creoles of the Acadians, as witness the "civilization" of Pouponne, the Parisian hero of *Tante Cydette*, written by a Paris-educated Creole, considers the locally educated Creoles as somewhat dull and indolent, and Dessommes makes fun of them presumably for the benefit of a Parisian audience. His appraisal coincides remarkably with George W. Cable's violently attacked views expressed in *The Grandissimes*. Tante Cydette accepted this hierarchy, too. She would marry her niece at any price, but she would marry her to a foreigner.

Our author shared with Cydalise Waldeck (Tante Cydette) the sense of upward mobility that characterized nineteenth-century America, but moved toward rather than away, as the majority did, from the Creole synthesis.

She praises the virtues of her heroine, but we are left with more than a suspicion that her greatest satisfaction is seeing Pouponne "Creolized."

Sidonie de la Houssaye's Works

A. Novels and long short stories

Pouponne et Balthazar. New Orleans: Librairie de *l'Opinion*, 1888.
Charles et Ella. Bonnet Carré [Reserve], La.: Imprimerie du *Meschacébé*, 1892.
Amis et fortune. Bonnet Carré, La.: Imprimerie du *Meschacébé*, 1893.

Published under the pseudonym of Louis Raymond

Les Quarteronnes de la Nouvelle-Orléans, Première Partie: Octavia la Quarteronne. Bonnet Carré, La.: Imprimerie du *Meschacébé*, 1894.
Les Quarteronnes de la Nouvelle-Orléans, Deuxième Partie: Violette la Quarteronne. Bonnet Carré, La.: Imprimerie du *Meschacébé*, 1895.

B. Serialized works in Louisiana newspapers

Le Mari de Marguerite. *L'Abeille* [New Orleans] (August 26-December 16, 1883).
La Dame au masque noir. *Le Franco-Louisianais* [New Orleans] (3rd installment running on May 14, 1887). [This one installment suggests a typical Southern romance.]
Charles et Ella. *Le Meschacébé* [Bonnet Carré, La.] (October 24, 1891-January 9, 1892).
Amis et Fortune. *Le Meschacébé* [Bonnet Carré, La.] (7th installment running on August 6, 1892).

Published under the pseudonym of Louise Raymond*

"Les Quarteronnes de la Nouvelle-Orléans, Deuxième Partie: Violetta la Quarteronne." *Le Meschacébé (6th installment running* on September 22, 1894).
"Les Quarteronnes de la Nouvelle-Orléans, Troisieme Partie: Gina La Quarteronne." *Le Meschacébé* (February 2, 1895-1897 (?)).
"Les Quarteronnes de la Nouvelle-Orleans, Quatrième Partie: Dahlia la Quarteronne." *Le Meschacébé* (May (?), 1897-July 30, 1898).

*Missing issues in the files of these newspapers make precise dating impossible in some cases.

C. Prize-winning allegory and idyll submitted to

L'Athénée Louisianais and published in its *Comptes Rendus*. "La Fauvette et le poète," *Comptes Rendus de l'Athénée Louisianais*, Livraison 3e, 4e série, tome 1 (May, 1890), 104-08.

"L'Amour qui renferme en lui seul tous les amours," *Comptes Rendus de l'Athénée Louisianais* (May, 1890), 108-12.

D. Miscellaneous

The Department of Archives of Louisiana State University Library has nineteen manuscript volumes totaling almost 5,100 pages. Short stories, children's stories, unpublished novels, translations from English, work copied from periodicals and several stories intended for sale to patent medicine companies as "testimonials" fill out the collection. The author alluded to other works as published, but in the absence of supporting evidence, they are not listed here.

Selected Bibliography

Books

Butcher, Philip. *George W. Cable*. New York: Twayne Publishers, Inc., 1962.

Cable, George W. *Strange True Stories of Louisiana*. New York: Charles Scribner's Sons, 1907.

Caulfield, Ruby Van Allen. *The French Literature of Louisiana*. New York: Columbia University Press, 1929.

Ditchy, Jay K. *Les Acadiens louisianais et leur parler*. Paris: Librairie E. Droz, 1932.

Fortier, Alcée. *Louisiana Studies*. New Orleans: F. F. Hansell and Bro., 1894.

Tinker, Edward Larocque. *Les Ecrits de langue française en Louisiane au XIXe siècle*. Paris: Librairie Anciene Honoré Champion, 1932.

Viatte, Auguste. *Histoire littéraire de l'Amérique française: Des origines à 1950*. Paris: Presses Universitaires de France, 1954.

Article

Perret, J. John. "*Strange True Stories of Louisiana*: History or Hoax?," *South-*

ern Studies, XVI, (1977), 41-53.

Dissertations and Theses

Savoie, Velma. "The Life and Writings of Sidonie de la Houssaye." (MA thesis, Louisiana State University, 1936).

Perret, J. John. "A Critical Study of the Life and Writings of Sidonie de la Houssaye with Special Emphasis on the Unpublished Works." (Ph. D. dissertation, Louisiana State University, 1966). [Extensive bibliography included.]

POUPONNE AND BALTHAZAR

I

May this little story give my readers the pleasure that it gave me in the past, when, seated on the knees of my grandmother, I would listen to it with attention, my gaze fixed on her blue eyes, that were so soft and intelligent and always beaming with love when fixed upon her daughter's children. The dear paralytic had this account from her mother, for at that far-off time, she had not yet been born. I will tell you but little of the political events which forced the Acadians to abandon fatherland and hearth in order to come establish themselves in a country so far from their own. I will talk to you of it at a later date while relating the adventures of Louis Comeau, the young hero, the noble leader, who at the price of all his fortune, extraordinary dangers and unspeakable fatigue, succeeded in leading several hundreds of Acadians to the banks of Bayou Tèche. Today, their descendants, the Comeaus, the Aucoins, the Boutets, the Moutons, the Broussards, the Bodins, the Leblancs, the Duprés, the Héberts, the Bérards and others whose names escape me, belong to the most distinguished families of the Attakapas and Opelousas countries, and certainly, not a single one has forgotten the precepts of honor, courage, energy and integrity bequeathed to them by their fathers, the worthy companions of Louis Comeau.

Louis Comeau and those who accompanied him were voluntary exiles fleeing the danger they foresaw, like the fisherman who seeks shelter from the storm he sees coming; but it wasn't the same for the unfortunates whom I am going to speak of to the reader. Later I will dwell on the causes of their exile, but for the moment, I will be satisfied with telling of the simple loves of Pouponne and Balthazar, both Acadians, both poor and without education, but good and above all full of confidence in the God whom they had learned to love from their earliest childhood.

Toward the end of the year 1762, my ancestor Pierre Bossier, married about three years, settled on a large piece of property that had been ceded to him by the government. This indigo plantation was situated on the banks of the Mississippi in the region of Louisiana called today Saint James Parish, but which at that time was only known as the Acadians. Why this name, one might ask? It is because in 1757, five years before Monsieur Bossier came to take possession of his land, a group of Acadians numbering two hundred and fifty (counting women and children) had come to form a colony in the midst of this beautiful countryside and had settled there for good. From time to time relatives and friends whom they had left behind came to join them, so that in 1762 our Acadians had there on the banks of the Mississippi a large village, or rather about fifty rural dwellings of different sizes, scattered about here and there, where they grew rice, indigo, cotton, sweet potatoes and especially corn. This colony which occupied about a dozen miles along the river had received the name of Little Acadia, but the people of Louisiana simply called it the Acadians. For years it kept this name and even today many Louisianians still say the Acadians when speaking of Saint James Parish.

It is said that the exiled Trojans used to give cherished names to the unknown places where they had gone to seek a new fatherland. At the time of which I spoke one saw arriving decimated families united by the same misfortune, driven away like the children of Ilium. These poor people stopped, as I have said, on the banks of the Mississippi at the spot where the old river seems to take pleasure in turning back on its course as if better to water the fertile plains it separates and to cool its waves under the shade of the giant oaks that shelter them. After many skirmishes with the Indians, after having penetrated the forest and drained the ground by herculean efforts, they settled there permanently. For them, the land which was going to soak up their sweat and tears, receive their last hopes, crown their old age and preserve their blessed remains, the land where their children were to be born and die, could have but one name. It must be called after the place where they had experienced all the delights life can give in the simple joys of their home during the beautiful days of illusions and mystery that delight every childhood here below. They did like those other pilgrims of the Italian peninsula; they named the corner of the earth they had just adopted Little Acadia, from the name of their lost fatherland. All exiles are brothers, whether victims of the Greeks or of the English, and the inspiration of misfortune everywhere has the same poetry of language.

If the first Acadians settled on the banks of the Teche had had to conquer almost insurmountable obstacles to arrive at their destination, they who had at their head a man of exceptional courage and energy, a man who had an immense personal fortune which he spent entirely to provide for the needs of his companions, think about what the second group of Acadians must have suffered, run off by the English and having as a leader only a poor priest whose voice was raised rather to console than to lead.

These poor families had come to Louisiana one after the [illegible] as debris of a shipwreck comes bit by bit to the same shore, when after many adverse winds, a continuous breeze starts to blow toward land. Brothers who had large families arrived with a few of their children or only with those of their neighbors. Maidens who had set out with their own parents made their way here with the parents of others. A man whose family included several brothers reached the end of his journey with two of his nephews; he never again heard from those who had stayed behind. A few friends, a few relatives succeeded in finding each other, but that was rare.

In the course of their peregrinations there were some who crossed incredible spaces on foot, through forests, along rivers and on barren seashores. Sometimes they were stopped by sickness and extreme poverty; at others they got lost for long periods. Some were asked to sell themselves as slaves or to shut themselves up in the coal mines of Pennsylvania; but they preferred to continue their way. They had run into a few of the agents whom Louis Comeau used to send to meet them, and they tried to rejoin their brothers. In addition they were looking for a friendly sky that would recall the one they were not to see again, and some died while looking for it.

When they arrived on the banks of the Mississippi at this beautiful site of which I spoke, the Acadians stopped, and though a few continued their way with the hope of rejoining the young leader who had sent agents to act as their guides, the Robicheaus, the Thériots, the Simoneaus, the Landrys and many others refused to go further and preferred to settle under this beautiful sky which recalled their absent homeland. Fr. Jacques, the worthy priest who had always walked at their head and who had shared so much of their deprivation and fatigue, resolved not to abandon his flock. It was with tears in his eyes that he saw the departure of those who were going to rejoin their brothers in Saint Martin Parish. He remained faithful to his post and continued to be the father, the leader of this flock that God, he said, had committed to his care.

II

My forebear with his noble and generous soul was quick to appreciate the worth of his neighbors. To be sure, he could not fail to notice their lack of education and their language, which at best could be called eccentric. But, what did this coarse external appearance matter to him? He intuitively grasped their lofty virtues, the honor and the energy hidden beneath this rough bark, and he lost no time in becoming better acquainted with them. He found a pleasure beyond words in hearing the injustices of which they were the object, their troubles and finally their long trips across the United States. Monsieur Bossier never laughed at the way this was told, and would come back the next day to his new friends who would say among themselves that this big *missié* was not at all *fiar* or conceited.

In 1762 my ancestor's family was still small. Monsieur Bossier came from French Flanders; he belonged to a rich and aristocratic family and had been simply indulging his taste for travel when he set out for America. On board the ship he met a young Viennese girl, Charlotte Blum, with whom he fell in love at first sight. Charlotte was coming to Louisiana to join her father, her only relative. Alas! upon arriving in New Orleans, the young girl learned that she was an orphan and that the elder Blum had died of yellow fever a few months before. Let us consider the dreadful position in which he was leaving the unfortunate girl without friends, without money and on a foreign soil whose language she did not even understand! It was then that, without hesitating, my forebear offered his hand to the one who already possessed his heart, and let us quickly say that he never had occasion to repent of this hasty union. Even if Charlotte, daughter of a simple artisan, did not have the outstanding advantages of education, if she had none of the elegant manners of the beautiful ladies of the time, she did become the faithful and devoted companion of the one she loved with all the strength of her being, of the one who later was to be the father of her ten children. An accomplished homemaker, thrifty, energetic, it is surely to her in large part that Pierre Bossier owed his immense fortune.

When he came to settle among the Acadians, Monsieur Bossier's family consisted of his wife, his two little daughters, Dorothée and Hélène, and of Placide, his young brother.

A year after his arrival in Louisiana, my ancestor, realizing the resources of his new country, did not want to be the only one to take advantage of them. He wrote to his father speaking with enthusiasm of his hopes and ended up by begging him to send him Placide, the youngest of his brothers, who had only just reached his eighteenth year. It was Placide himself who bore his father's answer. To be sure, the young man was far from having completed his studies, but his brother, instead of sending him to school, chose to keep him near him and personally took charge of his education.

At the time when this narrative opens, Placide was part of his brother's family. Intelligent and full of energy as the latter and brimming with self-confidence, he had a bright future opening before him; not only was he to be a member of the state legislature, but he would also have his name bestowed as a justly deserved honor on one of the finest parishes in the state. [Editor's note: The parish was in reality named after a later Pierre Bossier (1797-1845.)]

If Monsieur Bossier felt a lively attraction for his neighbors, the Acadians, Placide, while sharing this feeling, extended it to the fair sex and visited them more often, perhaps, than he should have. Handsome and glib, our young man was quite well received by the *Acadiennes*, and there was no dance or marriage to which *missié* Placide was not the first to be invited.

From the beginning, it was obvious that Madame Bossier in no way shared the feeling of her husband for the Acadians and still less that of her brother-in-law for the Acadian women.

When Charlotte arrived in Louisiana, she spoke only German, but she quickly learned French, which she studied with Pierre, who spoke it in the purest and most refined way, and who put in her hands books intended to make her best appreciate this beautiful language. And then, a few days after her arrival in Saint James, she witnessed a scene which we will tell you about later and which could only inspire in her disgust for women capable of using language so crude and common as that which she had heard.

Vainly her husband sought to dispose her more kindly toward them by relating to her the misfortunes of these hapless exiles; in vain did Placide make fun of her scruples and take pleasure in imitating the manners and speech of the *Cadiennes* in her presence. Charlotte would have none of it and would withdraw as soon as someone announced that an Acadian women was outside offering eggs and chicken for sale.

Good and generous as we know her to have been, she would see to it that all the chickens and eggs were bought and never refused the aid her neighbors so rarely sought. Let's concede that even if the Acadian is unpolished and uncouth, deep down inside he has all the pride of the aristocracy.

As noted earlier, the Acadians who had just settled on the banks of the Mississippi had as their leader a humble priest, a holy man whom everyone knew by the name of Fr. Jacques. Shut up aboard an enemy vessel with a few members of his flock, as he had been in the church at Grand Pré, cast out there upon the shores of Massachusetts, where he had rallied his flock around him, and as the shepherd starts to seek out the lost sheep, he started in search of his lost brothers in the midst of those unknown regions; he found a few of them, and setting out as their head he succeeded in leading them to this spot that he, as they, had adopted for their country. Fr. Jacques was a man of about fifty, strong and robust, and above all fully dedicated to the service of those whom he called his children. Upon his arrival in New Orleans, his first concern was to visit the bishop [Editor's note: There was no bishop in New Orleans until 1795.], and after telling his story, he had no difficlty in obtaining from him permission to spend the rest of his life among those whom he cherished like a father. The bishop, who was quite moved, handed over to Fr. Jacques at the moment when the latter was taking his leave, a sum of money intended to ease the first requirements of his congregation. The good priest complied with the bishop's wishes, but he held back from the gift he had received a small sum with which he had built a large cabin-like structure capable of holding three hundred people and which he called the church of Petite-Cadie. It was there that every Sunday in all kinds of weather the Acadians came to hear Mass and listen to the sermons of their worthy pastor.

Six miles from the Bossier plantation, this improvised church rose up in the very middle of the colony, and right next to it one saw the modest cabin, or rather the rectory, where Fr. Jacques lived with his old servant Pélagie and a young fellow of about twelve, called 'Tit Toine, who served as altar boy and took care of the pastor's rig.

It was in this cabin that every Sunday after Mass Fr. Jacques administered justice, for he was not only the priest, but also the chief magistrate of this little colony. It was he whom the Acadians came to consult in their quarrels and dissensions; and, indeed, his word was always listened to with respect and especially submission.

Monsieur Bossier and his brother had quickly learned to appreciate the noble instincts of this man of God, a saint at once unaffected and lofty; Charlotte herself felt a great respect for him and never failed to attend Mass. Quite often when the time came to get back in her carriage to return home, she would pass by the rectory to invite Fr. Jacques to dinner and would take him along with her, very proud to see him seated at her side and to be able to listen to his words, always filled with holy lessons and sage advice.

And always the fine priest had some touching anecdote to relate about these Acadians whom the young woman feared and avoided. One day she asked Fr. Jacques why he had left his country.

"Ah! *madame*," he said, "since our birth we were accustomed to consider the king of France our only sovereign, and all at once, they wanted to force us to swear allegiance to King George of England."

And as Charlotte was watching him with wide-open eyes, he continued:

"Yes, in order to force us to take, this oath by which the Acadians bound themselves to bear arms against France, this oath we had determined not to take, we soon became the object of all sorts of persecutions. The English considered us enemies and did not hesitate to treat us as such.

"One day a proclamation appeared posted in Grand Pré of which I was the pastor: here is the tenor of it:

> To the inhabitants of the district of Grand Pré, Minas Basin and Duck River–old men, young men and adolescents: His Excellency the governor having informed me of his decision relative to the inhabitants, and being desirous that each of them be fully informed of the intentions of His Majesty, order us to promulgate them such as they were committed to him: consequently, we order and strictly enjoin hereby all the inhabitants of the above-mentioned district, as well as the other districts, the old and the young, including children over ten years of age, to report to the church of Grand Pré, Friday the fifth of this month, at three in the afternoon, so that we may inform them of what we have been charged to communicate to them; declaring that no excuse under any pretense whatsoever will be accepted and that any disobedience will incur the confiscation of property and personal estate, in the absence of property.
>
> Given at Grand Pré, the second of September, 1757, in the 29th year of the reign of his Majesty.
>
> John Winslow

"What a memory you have, Fr. Jacques!" exclaimed Monsieur Bossier; "but continue, I beg you; your story interests us more than I can say."

The pastor smiled his sad smile and continued his narrative:

"As you can well imagine, this strange document produced a great sensation among the Acadians: they suspected danger, but did not realize its extent. Several of them went to my house, but not finding me in the rectory, they went to the house of old Landry: he was the patriarch of Grand Pré; his word, that of a man, as devout as he was honest, was always listened to with the most profound respect. Quite often Acadians came from the most remote villages to consult him. A great part of the inhabitants of Grand Pré did not know how to read; it was to have the proclamation read that they went out looking for me everywhere. They found me at old Landry's house where I had just gone in. The dignified patriarch handed me the paper asking to have it read aloud, for he, like the others, was destitute of all education. You can imagine the emotions that the reading stirred in the souls of those who were listening to me. All had something to say: several affirmed that a treacherous act was concealed beneath these promises of the English. Others spoke of hidden mysteries and asked for what purpose the children were summoned to this assembly;

and why a Friday, an unlucky day, had been chosen.

"'Ah!' they cried, 'there is something diabolical in all that. We must arm and resist, or we must flee, and like Louis Comeau go look elsewhere for a new country to call our own.'

"The agitation was indescribable when old Landry stood up: then silence came over the room. Everything in this man of eighty-four commanded respect: he had twenty sons and grandsons in the group and had nothing to gain by creating illusions for himself or empty hopes for others. All in Grand Pré loved and venerated him. He had the appearance and character of a patriarch and was treated with the same respect as a pastor. Here are his thoughts, but in my words:

> My children, you come to me to seek advice in the difficult position where we find ourselves. Ah! I dare hope that you will accept without hesitation the course of action that my heart tells me to recommend, for it is truly the only thing left for us to do. We are today subjects of England; we must submit to England, which, after all, is a noble nation incapable of treachery. You speak of resisting? What means do you have to do it? We don't have a single weapon and no means of getting ourselves any. We are surrounded by English forts and soldiers, and at the first movement, at the first cry of revolt, we would be exterminated. Others talk about fleeing, of following the example of Louis Comeau? Fleeing? . . . How? . . . Where? . . . The country is guarded on all sides; we don't have a single small boat. When Louis Comeau left Acadia, he did it openly; then the roads were open and he took away with him immense resources. But us? The English fleet is guarding our coasts and the sea itself is closed to us. Why should we on the brink of winter go wandering about the woods with our wives and children in search of a new home that we will never be able to reach? I repeat it to you, my children, submission is imposed upon us. Let us meet, therefore, in the church of Grand Pré, as our superiors order; let us walk fearlessly under the protection of our worthy pastor. If any evil befalls us, we will only be the victims of it, for we are not guilty. God has pity on those who suffer; he only punishes those who cause suffering. He will be on our side.

These words produced a great effect: they were full of good sense. The respectful silence with which they listened continued. With downcast eyes each one made his way towards the door stopping en route to shake the hand of the venerable old man.

IV

The following day around noon nearly two thousand people had gathered in the little village of Grand Pré. Many had come from a rather great distance with all their families. All were grouped in front of the houses on the main street next to the church. Most were busy dispatching a light meal which they ate while standing. There was no uproar: one would have said that a gloomy veil covered this crowd over which a veritable stupor reigned. People talked in a low voice as when one gets ready to commit the mortal remains of a friend or brother to the tomb. One felt, one sensed calamity.

"When the old clocks which had marked so many happy moments in these remote cottages began to strike three, all felt their hearts tighten, the groups gave a start, and at the same moment the rolling of a drum was heard in the direction of the priest's house: it was the signal announcing the opening of the meeting. Immediately the whole population started to move. Most of the members of a family kept together. Here and there one saw a few white-haired villagers around whom were gathering the representatives of several generations grouped by age. It seemed as though they were the patriarchs of the Israelites making their way to the plains of the promised land. A few women, a few girls, eager to know the result of this great and mysterious affair, had also mixed in the mass of men.

"The women were not allowed to enter the church; the guards placed on the steps crossed their bayonets in front of them. And when the last of this long procession of men had entered and when the little place of worship was full of those it had seen praying and singing as late as last Sunday, they saw Winslow, Butler and Murray advancing and surrounded by a guard with drawn swords. All three crossed the threshold of the church and after opening their way through the midst of the assembly, they stopped on the steps of the altar. The door closed behind them and a double row of soldiers encircled the church, closing it in a double belt of sharpened bayonets.

"But pardon, *madame* and you my friends," said Fr. Jacques interrupting his story. "I am afraid to let myself get carried too far away by memories and thus bore you."

"Bore us, Fr. Jacques!" cried Charlotte while clasping her hands. "No, you can not imagine the interest your story has for us! Continue, I beg you!"

The good priest turned toward my ancestor as if to ask his opinion.

"Your words, father," answered Monsieur Bossier, "have as compelling an interest for me as for my wife, and I would be heartbroken if you did not finish this story, which makes my heart beat with pity and indignation."

"Oh! yes, continue!" added Placide.

"A dreadful silence settled everywhere inside," continued the priest. "Winslow, although a decisive man, appeared overwhelmed by it: he hesitated a few moments to break it, turning the fateful parchment over and over in his hands; Murray and Butler, too, seemed to share his pity. Finally Colonel Winslow made an effort and put together these few sentences:

> Gentlemen, I have received from His Excellency Governor Lawrence this dispatch from the king. You have been brought together in order to become acquainted with His Majesty's latest decision. It is with profound sorrow that I see myself forced to make it known to you. Here it is: namely, that your lands, your furnishings and real property, your animals of all types, in short, all that you possess, except your clothes and money, is hereby declared property of the crown, and in addition His Majesty orders that you be expelled from this province.

"'You see', continued the colonel, 'the will of the king is that the French population of this district of which you are a part be driven from it forever.'"

"Heavens!" cried Charlotte, "is such an injustice possible?"

"All that I am telling you is true, *madame*," answered Fr. Jacques. "Winslow continued by assuring the wretched Acadians that he would see to it that the families were not separated and promised that they would be put aboard the same ship. He added that the dispatch of His Majesty further specified that they were to remain prisoners until the time that they were ready to be loaded on the ships.

"These words produced a general disturbance. Like the first effort of a volcano that suddenly erupts, there escaped from these burdened bosoms a heartrending cry, full of anguish and of sobs: it was the cry of crushed hearts, of a thousand victims hit by the same blow. All these poor people, suddenly struck, felt themselves instinctively turned toward the one from whom the blow came. As shipwrecked people, under whose feet the depths of the ocean had just opened, with the instinct of self-preservation, rush toward the rock that caused their ruin, all arms were simutaneously raised toward Winslow, imploring without words, but with stifled cries with a heartrending despair . . . . But the sentence was carried out; the sacrifice was to be made.

"Winslow, Murray and Butler went down the altar steps. The swords of their guards kept at a distance the imploring arms and the heaving chests as the three executioners somberly passed by, seemingly calm and cold."

Charlotte sobbed and Placide made great efforts to control his emotion.

"Outside when the women heard the frightful exclamations of their fathers, husbands and children, they felt a shiver to the very depths of their souls; their tender instincts drew them all toward the entrance of the church and they waited in indescribable anxiety for the moment when the door would open. When they saw it ajar, they rushed toward it, but it was Winslow, Murray and Butler leaving with their sycophants. They told the women to withdraw; they did not budge; they pushed them back with their hands and threatened them with their swords, but they opposed the steel with their bodies and suffered blows on the head in order to be able to stretch out their arms to those whom they could glimpse through the opening in the door."

"Oh! those noble heroines!" exclaimed Charlotte.

"You won't run away from them anymore?" asked her husband.

"Oh! be quiet, Pierre!" cried the blushing young lady; "I did not know."

Fr. Jacques continued: "They backed up only when they saw Butler turn the key in the lock.

"Ah! who will ever be able to comprehend and weigh the sorrows that the night which followed this catastrophe hid in its darkness? . . . all those families without heads, those weak and sickly women without bread-winners, all those mothers deprived of their joys, their pride, their love . . . all those empty places by the fireside, in the beds of spouses . . . all the sweet gaiety of the evening gatherings suddenly gone . . . all the kisses in the evening one was no longer to receive, the sweet laughter of children that one was no longer to hear! And with all that were mixed horrible visions and hideous nightmares . . . God alone has seen all, heard all!

"The departure of the Acadians was fixed for the tenth, and Winslow had the prisoners notified. Five vessels were waiting for them, or rather, were expected at any time.

"Then just for one day they released ten of the prisoners so they could help their wives get supplies ready for the exile. Ten others replaced them the next day, but alas! some thirty at the very most were able to take advantage of this permission: two days only separated them from the time of departure.

"I told you that Winslow had promised the Acadians that the families would not be separated, and yet, without seeming to recall this promise, the soldiers first pushed forward the young men and children, then the old men; then the women were thrown (that expression is the only accurate one) randomly aboard these vessels, without knowing whom they would find . . . . Oh! it was frightful! frightful!"

The priest stopped to catch his breath. Charlotte, her face hidden in her hands, was weeping hot tears. Placide, like his brother, no longer sought to hide his emotion.

"*Madame*," said Fr. Jacques after a moment, "allow me to set before you two very touching episodes that occurred at the time of departure of my ill-fated compatriots."

"Weren't you with them, father?" asked the young woman as she raised her head.

"Yes, my child, they put me among the old men: why? I don't know, unless it was aid and console them in their abandonment."

V

"When our men received the order to head toward the ships that they could see close by, they obeyed without murmuring, full of confidence in the word of the colonel, who, if you recall, had promised that the families would not be separated and would leave together.

"The young men and the [male] children were put in front in rows of six, and the old men, placed after them in the same order, were calmly awaiting the colonel's order to proceed toward the coast. All were resigned; not a single exclamation arose from the midst of that crowd; they were expecting that their mothers, their wives and their daughters would come to join them in a few moments and they did not even think of bidding them farewell.

"But Butler soon came to stir up a storm in these pacified hearts by commanding the young men and children to move out by themselves in the direction of the ships.

"'You must get on before your relatives,' he said.

"'No' No' all cried out, 'we do not want to leave without them . . . we won't budge from here unless they follow us . . . Why separate us? . . . do you see those children? Can they do without their mothers? We are ready to obey, but with them . . . our relatives, our fathers, our mothers, our wives! . . . They must leave with us!'

"At the same time they turned around to go mingle with the rows of old men; but this cry from the depths of the soul had been forseen and they found behind them a barrier of soldiers that they could not force and before which they stopped, still protesting with the same steadfastness.

"Butler shouted to his men to advance on them and move them at the end of their weapons. These despicable men were just waiting for such an order to satisfy their cruelty. They rushed at them, then, directing these sheaves of bayonets at these bosoms too full of love, at these arms upraised to heaven, at these poor unarmed people who only sought a paternal embrace. The blood of these children (there were some among them who had barely finished their tenth year) flowed before their mothers, before their old relatives, who were holding out their arms to them, but upon seeing why they were being wounded, begged them to go away without them.

"'Leave, children!' shouted old Landry, 'God will watch over us!'

"The poor old man had six sons, eight sons-in-law and sixteen grandchildren in this group of victims.

"They obeyed and took their places again, this time calm in appearance, but despairing. And at the end of a moment the holds of the ships were swallowing up their first loads of martyrs.

"Then it was the turn of the old men. It was the same heartrending spectacle: the same scenes of grief accompanied them, only their march was more silent. By the movement of their lips one guessed that they were praying. They were advancing slowly, bent by age and despair, counting their last steps on this land that they had watered with their sweat. Several were bareheaded, as if they believed themselves on the road to Calvary. Devoted patriarchs, they bade farewell to the happy birthplace that they had prepared for these generations which had come as a blessing from heaven and whom they were now going to lead on the road of exile. The poor women, beside themselves with despair, watched them move away, and it seemed that their hearts would burst asunder.

"At the head of this funeral-like procession walked old Landry, bent over the staff on which he leaned with both hands. The old man's sons who had just embarked were not his only sons: over and above his daughters and daughters-in-law, he had four sons who had been settled for some years with their families on the Bay of Beau Bassin where they had fine places. But, when the troubles began, when the English troops walked the streets of Grand Pré, old Landry, frightened about the safety of his children, sent Balthazar, his youngest son, to the Bay of Beau Bassin in order to warn his brothers of the danger that was threatening the country. He advised them to take what they could carry, leave their homes with their children and try to reach a land where they would have nothing to fear, and where, later, they could be reunited, the father with his children.

"Balthazar was a handsome young man of about twenty, good, intelligent, strong and always first in all physical activities. He was engaged to Pouponne

Thériot, the most beautiful girl in Grand Pré. She was not yet fifteen, and it had been decided (before the troubles, of course) that her marriage would take place on her next birthday. Pouponne, seeing the children of the village embark, thanked God, who had allowed Balthazar and Périchon Thériot, her brother, to be absent at this terrible moment. In order not to travel alone, Balthazar had taken along with him his fiancée's brother, a boy of seventeen.

"'Alas!' poor Pouponne was saying to herself in the midst of her tears, 'I will probably never see them again!'

"While the column of old men was advancing, Pouponne was standing in the midst of a group of women whom she was trying to console and supported her mother, poor woman, who herself looked despairingly at the ship that was to take her three eldest sons far from her. The unfortunate woman seemed to have forgotten everything in this silent contemplation; she was not listening to Pouponne and paid no attention to the little twins clinging to her dress.

"At the moment when the old men were going to set foot on the gangplank that led to the ship, old Landry stopped as if to say a last farewell to those who were around him. Driven by anger, a soldier gave a violent push to the old man, who would have fallen, if Pouponne, who had seen everything, had not rushed to his aid and caught him in her arms. Exasperated by this unexpected help, the soldier leaped toward the couple, and before the girl understood his intention, before Madame Thériot noticed the disappearance of her daughter, the soldiers pushed the old man and the girl as though they formed but a single body, and Pouponne found herself on the ship before she had the time to realize what had happened. Alas! in vain the poor child tried to soften the hearts of her tormentors by showing them her despairing mother, in vain did I try to join my entreaties to hers; all was to no avail! Pouponne Thériot had just seen her mother for the last time."

"Oh! it's hideous!" cried Charlotte while shuddering pulling even more closely to her bosom the brown head of little Dottée, who at the moment was seated on her mothers' knees.

"When the heroic child had tried everything," continued the prest, "when she had entreated the monsters who were surrounding her, she understood that all was useless and she arose strong and outwardly calm, dried her eyes, and moving toward old Landry:

"'Father of Balthazar,' she said, 'it is God, who sent me to you. You will be my father . . . and I, beginning at this moment, become your daughter.'

"And kneeling before the old man: 'Give me your blessing, father!' she said.

"And with his arms outstretched over this angelic head, old Landry from the heart adopted the child who had just dedicated herself to him. And I tell you, *madame*, this noble girl has worthily carried out this self-imposed mission . . . she is indeed the child of her fiancé's father; she cares for him, loves him and consoles him with all the zeal and tenderness of a real daughter."

"Fr. Jacques," asked Madame Bossier with emotion, "is Pouponne here? does she belong to your flock?"

"Yes, my child, and she is its sweet protectress, its guardian angel. Her charity has no limits and can be compared only to her devotion. Ah! she is truly our Sister of Charity . . . you always find her by the sickbed, wherever care and consolation are to be afforded . . . I repeat, *madame*, she is our Providence."

"She is rich then?"

"Rich! the poor child doesn't have a penny: she has nothing to give but her care and her nights spent with the sick. If a mother needs to go out, she does not hesitate to send her children to Pouponne, and Pouponne teaches them their prayers and talks to them of the good God who watches over them. If there is a sick person, the first thing is to send for Pouponne. Ah! *madame*! if you have a charity to dispense, find this young saint and she will point out those who need it. But, for herself, she refuses everything, remember that . . . she is as proud as she is good."

"'Thank you for your story, Fr. Jacques," said Charlotte, "tomorrow I will go see Pouponne. And what about old Landry?"

"He lives with Pouponne in the second cabin of the settlement, a stone's throw from your house. This kind girl has faithfully kept her promises: she cares for him with the tenderness and devotion of a real daughter. The old man adores her. Besides, with the exception of her young brother 'Tit Toine, whom I had the luck to find upon arriving in Massachusetts, old Landry is the only relative Pouponne has here, and at that, a relative of her fiancé."

"'Fr. Jacques," asked Charlotte with a certain hesitation, "does Pouponne have the same manners and speech of the other Acadians?"

Now it was the priest who hesitated: "Like her companions, Pouponne has no education and doesn't even know how to read, but she is gifted with an instinctive modesty that directs all her actions. In the midst of crude and unrefined beings, she is neither unrefined nor crude. Moreover she is very timid and does not talk much; certainly the expressions she uses are not elegant, but they are never offensive or tasteless. She is very religious and I have often seen her blush while listening to the oaths and rough language of our Acadians."

"'Fr. Jacques," said Charlotte, "I am ashamed of having stayed so long without visiting my neighbors. I have sinned through pride; I acted like Pouponne; I blushed while hearing them curse and blaspheme and I made a whole population responsible for the faults of a single person. Placide will tell you what happened to me and you will excuse me, or so I hope! No later than tomorrow, I repeat, I will go see Pouponne."

"You can help her in her need, for the poor child in indeed in want, obliged as she is to support her adopted father. Don't offer her any money, as that would be a great humiliation for her. But give her some work; she sews well and weaves splendid cotton cloth. In addition to that she sells chickens and eggs."

"Thank you for your remarks. I will know how to act," replied my ancestress.

Fr. Jacques concluded: "As I see that you are interested in the fate of my protegée, when I come back again, I will tell you what I know of the love story of Pouponne and Balthazar."

"Let's hope that you don't make me wait too long for your next visit," said Charlotte, "for you have certainly guessed that without knowing Pouponne, I already feel like her friend."

VI

We are now going to describe a scene that had taken place several months before and which had given Charlotte a real fright arousing the enmity that her neighbors, the Acadian women, inspired in her.

Madame Bossier rarely left home and devoted herself entirely to the duties of the household and more especially to the attention that her two girls in their infancy demanded. At that remote time the job of a housewife was no sinecure, far from it. The country folk who desired to set a good table and worthily exercise the duties of hospitality were obliged to do everything themselves and to raise everything on their own plantations. Today when money does everything, it is difficult for us to realize the genuine labors of Hercules of our ancestors, who liked to enjoy life as we do, even at the cost of much effort. Let's take the Bossier plantation for example, and let us speak of the immense herds of pigs, of the flocks of sheep and goats entrusted to the care of a half-dozen Negroes too old to work in the fields; let's glance at the immense vegetable garden and the huge orchard filled with all sorts of fruit. Two women and several pickaninnies took care of the pigeon house and the poultry yard, which was Charlotte's pride, and the dairy, too. Over and above the hams, cheeses, syrups, jams and preserved foods of all sorts which were made on the plantation under the eyes of its mistress; my forebear employed two hunters and two fisherman whose duty it was to furnish game and fish for the master's table.

In addition to the household work, she had to supervise the looms for cotton (the cloth with which they clothed the slaves) and look in occasionally on the plantation hospital put in the care of several old black women, for if Charlotte was a good mother, let us also acknowledge that she was the best of mistresses.

As we see, the young woman had little time to give to visiting; moreover, she did not have a single relative in Louisiana and had not yet had the time to make many friends there.

On a beautiful May afternoon Placide entered his sister-in-law's room and suggested that she come with him on a walk on the main road which followed the Mississippi. Charlotte accepted without hesitating and after entrusting her children to their old nurse, she quickly put on a lace mantilla and went out with her young brother-in-law.

It was a Sunday and at each step our strollers ran into groups of Acadians in their Sunday best on the road or enjoying the fresh air in front of the fence which surrounded their house, their backs leaning against the fence and their feet hanging in the ditch. It wasn't the first time that Charlotte had seen her neighbors, but in spite of everything, she could not prevent herself from looking at them with curiosity. For many of these poor people, the only luxury they allowed themselves on Sunday was cleanliness. They had just about forgotten the practice of wearing shoes. They were all dressed in blue or yellow cotton outfits made by their wives. During the week their dress was a sort of pants and a jumper; but on Sunday the jumper was replaced by a round vest they called a *capot*. Their hats were made from palmetto leaves and were also their wives' handiwork.

As for the women, they showed a little more stylishness than their husbands; the cotton dresses were put aside on Sunday and replaced by a cloth that was lighter and brilliantly colored. The women whom Charlotte passed were all dressed very much alike; a very short skirt, red, orange, green or blue and a *caraco* (a very short basque) all covered with buttons and opening on a pleated blouse. Around their necks they wore enormous necklaces of colored glass beads and on their ears large rings of gold, copper or of colored beads matching their necklaces. Some had shoes, but very few. Nearly all were bare-headed, allowing their hair to fall in plaits on their shoulders; others wore the traditional sunbonnet and others still had covered their hair with a colored kerchief tied under the chin. As for the children, all were almost half-naked.

And our Acadians opened their eyes wide in amazement upon seeing the wife of the *gros missie*, as they called my forebear, and in their astonishment they forgot to greet her. As for Placide, he was known by all in this little community, whose friend he had become by participating in their dances and celebrations. The Acadian gossip went so far as to say that he had a favorite among the girls of Petite-Cadie. And indeed the young man from Flanders had shown his good taste by courting the charming 'Tite Mine, a girl of fourteen who was rightly recognized as the prettiest in the settlement.

But if 'Tite Mine received with a smile the attention and presents of the young man, if she was proud to have him for a partner at the Saturday dances, and lastly if his visits were received with pleasure by the young Acadian girl, her mother was certainly not of the same mind. By her masculine and quarrelsome mannerisms Terencine had succeeded in making herself the terror of the settlement. She was very tall and dark-complexioned; her angular lines, her stiff gait, her heavy eyebrows gave her the look of a man dressed as a woman; especially since her hair which was like a mattress was always covered with a man's hat. Honesty compels us to say that the mother of pretty 'Tite Mine was as disgusting as she was repulsive. Add to what I have just said a voice that made itself heard a mile away, the crudest language one can imagine, and we will not be amazed to hear that Terencine was a domineering woman, who allowed no one in the family to raise his voice before her. Her husband, Theogene Simoneau, a little bit of a man, was the first to set the example of submission. People went so far as to say that his wife used a whip on him. Anyway, she was certainly capable of such a thing.

In the beginning Terencine had received Placide's visits with pleasure: she took obvious pride while speaking of the gold rings and beautiful ribbons that he had given to 'Tite Mine; but if our virago was brusque and uncouth, she was respectable, and seeing that the young man never spoke of marriage, she had a terrible scene with her daughter, went so far, they say, as to beat her, and ended up by forbidding her to speak to this smooth-talking seducer of girls who had sugar on his lips and vinegar in his heart.

'Tite Mine cried, but as Placide was obliged to be away for a few days, she had not been able to communicate her mother's orders to him.

As we must assume, Placide, a born and bred aristocrat, was only looking for a short-lived distraction with this sweet Acadian girl. The thought of marrying this common person would never have come to his mind. But deep in his heart the young man admitted that his conduct was not very commendable, and he was careful not to speak of 'Tite Mine Simoneau to his brother and less to his sister-in-law, whose extreme delicacy and noble feelings he knew.

VII

And now all of a sudden our strollers found themselves in the presence of this dreadful Térencine at the moment when she was going home. The Simoneau house was built on the road and was not surrounded by any fence as were all the other cabins of the settlement. Our virago got up God knows how in her Sunday best was holding a basket of eggs. Upon seeing her, Placide brought his hand to his hat and greeted her with these words:

"Good day, Madame Théogène."

"Good day," she replied in a voice that augured nothing good.

Placide, who wanted to amuse Charlotte, stopped.

"How much for your eggs?" he asked.

"A bit an' a 'alf," she replied with a surly tone.

"It's too much," he said.

He was trying to make her talk and succeeded only too well.

"Ah! eets like dat!" she said, "well you won' 'ave 'em for de way you talk about 'em."

"One bit and I'll take everything," said Placide.

At that moment a woman still young but prematurely aged by poverty and misfortune, appeared on the porch of the cabin. She had her bosom completely uncovered and was nursing an infant. Térencine turned toward her while Charlotte blushed and turned her head away.

"Well speak up, Maré-Jeanne!" shouted the virago. "You got for sell dis gen'lman fo' one bit? Mister, where you live? I'm gone send 'em by de cousin of ma dog."

And each of these words was accented with a deep bow.

Placide was holding his sides from laughter.

"What reason you got for laugh like dat?" she shouted; "you 'alf a lil' man! Wit a dead man face dat make ma cat trow up . . . but . . . look how he open dat mout! Get out here! quick . . . quick . . . or I put you head on backside front."

"Placide . . . I beg you! let's go!" said Charlotte in German.

"In a minute," he answered in the same language; "there is nothing to fear."

"Well! Well!" cried Térencine, "deh, dey talkin' Latin jus' like a pries'. You say Mass, too, m'am?"

"Madame Théogène," continued Placide, "do you want to fight? . . . well, I am your man . . . come on! It will be the two of us." An he started to roll up his sleeves.

"Placide!" implored Charlotte as she clung to her brother-in-law's arm.

"You!" cried our fishwife, "you mess up carcass! Why wit one slap I nail down you soul 'tween two pave stone . . . You betta believe me, you, de devil's own *boudin*, you *coquin* fo' sho! Get out here. I put a mark to you eye so you see nottin' but black for leas' six week."

"If I were a coward, old woman," said Placide, "you would indeed frighten me."

Térencine was really wound up and the "old woman" added to her exasperation.

"Who you call old woman, you *modèle* for all good-for-nottin'? I'm more pretty still dan lots of de lady who cause dey dress fine tink dey got right for look down on poor folk."

My ancestress, understanding that they were talking of her, pressed more insistently on her companion's arm; she dared not speak after Térencine asked her if she said Mass.

As Placide was having a good time, he seemed unaware of his sister-in-law's terror.

"Ah! Madame Théogène," he said, "you are wrong to get all worked up . . . you are as red as a poppy and . . . pleurisy has been very dangerous this year."

God knows what she would have answered if at that very moment 'Tite Mine, attracted by the noise, had not appeared on the gallery. The child was really charming with her red skirt and her little black velvet *caraco* all decorated with bows of red ribbons; the laced bodice, as well as the gold rings and the cross she wore hanging from a black velvet ribbon, were gifts from Placide.

On seeing him, she smiled and showed two rows of the prettiest white teeth that a duchess would have envied.

Charlotte was looking admiringly at the young girl and her picturesque costume, but the sight of her drove Térencine to a paroxysm of exasperated rage: she sounded like an enraged hyena.

"What you come for do here, you ugly boy-chaser?" she shouted.

And before the child had time to answer, she jumped on the gallery and, taking her daughter by the arm, she threw her with all her strength through the half-opened door. While all that was going on, Théogène Simoneau, a little bit of a man who barely came up to Térencine's shoulder, was calmly seated at the end of the gallery and never for a moment took his eyes from the piece of wood that he was carving with the knife he had in his hand.

'Tite Mine was making the house reverberate with her cries and Charlotte, trembling with fright, was pleading with Placide to withdraw. Térencine, her fists clenched, was advancing toward the young man who, exasperated by her conduct toward her daughter, was standing his ground. But on hearing 'Tite Mine's cries, she stopped . . . and addressing herself to her daughter-in-law who had just appeared on the gallery:

"Maré-Jeanne," she yelled, "for why she cry like dat?"

"Eet's dat she done fall down," replied Marie-Jeanne.

Placide did not know what to do: he saw Charlotte's paleness and fright, and deep down he feared for her, but run from Térencine, oh! that was impossible! She advanced on him with fists upraised.

"Now," she said, "you low-down, sweet-talk girl fooler! dirty pig snout! If you dare pass here again, I gone put a hit on you nose dat can flat it good on you face and make eet sick for de res' of you life . . . Ah! you come sweet-talk my girl, you make her for go run roun' wit you. Ah! you ain't nottin' but coward for try fool a girl dat age! An' eef it not be for de lady deh, I hit you head so eet don' look no betta."

Turning her back to him, Térencine went back in the house with a certain dignity. The last words our strollers heard were those that she addressed to her daughter: "You gone stop cry like dat? In a minute I close dat big mout, you girl wid no heart! Ah! so dat's what you learn at catechis' for let yousef be make love to dat Placide."

And Placide, who did not want to abandon his last attack on his antagonist, shouted as he was going away:

"*Au revoir*, Térencine! You really give the impression of being drunk

. . . be so kind as to present my compliments to *mamzelle* 'Tite Mine."

She would not condescend to reply. They went away in silence. Charlotte still trembling, and Placide, thinking about 'Tite Mine, genuinely regretted this distraction Térencine had given him and which he now hoped not to continue.

As I said, Charlotte upon leaving home had covered her head with a lace mantilla. While passing near a group of women, she heard one of them make the following remark:

"Look deh what she got on her head! Eet look like calf gut, all dem fol' an pleat what she pile up on her head."

We must admit that Charlotte had good reasons not to admire the Acadian women. When they were a little distance away, she gently began to scold her brother-in-law, pointing out the thoughtlessness and lack of discretion in his conduct; but he reassured her, affirming that he had never spoken a word of love to 'Tite Mine.

"I admit that I danced with her," he added, "that I took her to dances several times . . . . Out of pity for her extreme poverty, I gave her a few small gifts . . . that's all!"

"Well! believe me," said Charlotte, "stay at that point; don't go any further, for this horrible Térencine creature could give you trouble and perhaps ill-treat her daughter."

VIII

The following day according to her promise made to Fr. Jacques, Charlotte started out early taking along in her carriage a basket filled with provisions for old Landry. Few women were gifted with as fine a sensibility as my ancestress: she could intuitively feel the pain or humilation she might cause and did everything to avoid it. Thus, she said to herself, that if she went straight to Pouponne's house, the latter could guess that the priest had spoken of her, and she would suffer from this indiscretion. Consequently, she had her carriage stopped in front of the first cabin, that of the families of the brothers Théodule and Gaspard Labauve, of whom she heard nothing but good. She did not dare get down, but ordered her driver to call out. At that time all the men were in the fields, and Charlotte from her carriage could see in the back of the yard two women busy doing the washing, while a flock of children, one dirtier and more ragged than the other, were wallowing in the mud with pigs and ducks that filled the yard. While her driver was calling out at the top of his lungs, Madame Bossier was looking over the house in front of her and wondering how eighteen people could live in it. She had been told that the two brothers, their old mother, and their thirteen children all lived together.

In answer to the driver's shouting, an old woman appeared on the gallery. She was quite tall and her large frame, still erect, was supported by a staff on which she was leaning with both hands. She was dressed in a flowing garment made of light cotton and her long white hair hanging on her shoulders was fluttering in the wind. It was the grandmother of the family, and on seeing her, Charlotte got down and went to the fence. She greeted the old woman with respect, and the latter in turn greeted her, and asked in a high-pitched voice:

"What can ah do for hep you, m'am?"

"I would like to buy some chickens and eggs," replied Madame Bossier.

The old woman started to laugh: "Dey don' know me no mo', de chicken," she said, "*mais* 'scuse me, ah gon' call mah son's wife; she talk more betta dan me."

And going back in the house, one heard her call:

"Zozo! eh! Zozo! Titine! where you, you lazy people?"

A voice answered from the farthest part of the yard:

"What eet is, *mère*?"

"Come, and ah tell you . . . a lady all dress fine, and she want buy some chicken."

"Good, *mère*, ah m'a come."

And Zozo hurried to wipe her hands covered with soapsuds, and after exchanging a few words with Titine, she made her way toward Charlotte who was then leaning on the fence.

One thing is to be noted; an Acadian is not timid and speaks his mind in front of anybody; neither wealth nor station impresses him, and he will speak with as much familiarity before a princess as before a girl watching turkeys.

Zozo was barefooted and had nothing on her head to protect it from the sun but a blue cotton kerchief tied under her chin. My great-grandmother, was, as usual, quite simply dressed in a brown wool dress covered with a heavy-weight tartan throw (they called it an Angora shawl) and a simple head covering of black silk; but for these poor people who were scrutinizing her, she was dressed in an unheard of luxury, or "all dress fine," as the old grandmother had just said. But Zozo did not even seem to notice it and approached the fence through which the conversation took place.

"Good day, madame," said Charlotte polite as ever, "excuse me for having disturbed you, but a disease broke out among my chickens and I find myself having to buy some more. Can you sell me a few dozen?"

"Dat depen, m'am," said our Acadian, "eet's for eat dem you want dese animal?"

"But of course," said Charlotte a little astonished.

"I gon' tell you for why ah axe you dat; eef you gon' raise dem, well! no deal an' ah don' make you happy. Ah raise pretty much chicken dis year an' not one die sick, *mais de chorus*, dem dey don' make, an' on tree dozen female, ah got only two *chorus*, dat suit you?"

Charlotte understood what she meant, but it must be said that it was the first time that he heard the word *chorus* applied to roosters.

"Very well, madame," she said, "I will take the three dozen chickens, although I would like to have more. And what is the price?"

"One *pias*' (dollar) de dozen for de chicken and one bit for de egg. Dat suit you, m'am?"

"Certainly," replied Charlotte, "get the chickens ready; I am going a little further down the road and I will pick them up on the way back, with all the eggs you can spare."

At that moment two boys dressed only in shirts ran up while arguing and calling to their mother for help.

"Those are your children, madame?" asked Charlotte, "how they look alike!"

"Nottin' surprise 'bout dat, dey was *bezons*." The word *bezons* she used for twins was also new to Charlotte.

"Who lives in the first house?" asked my ancestress feigning ignorance in the hope of hearing about Pouponne.

"Some fine people," answered the Acadian woman, "ol' Landry an' his girl. Dass Pouponne, she's a lamb her, God's bes'!"

"An angel," said the vistor in turn.

"An' wid dat, so sad!" continued Zozo. "Poor ting! She lost all in one minute. It make five year dat she wait for her beau an' all her broder . . . as for de *maman*, for sho' she mus' be dead now. Ah! m'am! If you be able to see our Pouponne in de ol' day . . . she was de mos' pretties' girl in place . . . an' now, she so doggone sad, and when she tink dat she by hersef she cry so make you heart turn inside out; jus' like her black eye so nice befo', dat you say dey's two diamond, today dey look like de eye of an ol' white rabbit.

An' de wose ees dat de poor ting hide her troub', dat she swallow eet down . . . nottin' but dat! an' she turn white, yellow like de sick people, she turn green, dat you look at her, eet make you sick inside, an' if Balthazar waste mo' time for get himsef here, dat poor lil' ting gon' be dead for sho'.

IX

At the moment when Charlotte was going to get back in her carriage, she stopped, surprised and amused at a little scene that was taking place a few steps from her. A little boy of about twelve, freckled like a turkey egg, having for his only clothes a long shirt, was approaching all out of breath from pursuing a sow that did not want to join the herd in spite of the blows from the whip with which Zozo's son was attacking it, with *hu's*! and *ho's*! given at the top of his lungs. Upon hearing him the old grandmother, still standing on the gallery, shouted at him without altering her position:

"Dass you, Baptiste?"

"Yes, *mère*," he replied.

"Well, you find dat sow an' her lil' pig?"

"Yes, *mère*," answered the child again, "dey dere."

Zozo raised her hands in a gesture of horror.

"Oh! madame," she cried out, "'scuse dat chil'! Dat ting talk French like a black man." And turning toward her son:

"*Sacré Bambara*!" she said, "for why don' you say: Dey *are* dere, *grand-mère*?"

And the child repeated: "Dey *are* dere, *grand-mère*."

It was laughing to the point of tears that Charlotte described this scene to her husband and Placide.

Pouponne's house was just a few steps from the Labauve's, and she felt moved and disturbed in spite of herself while telling herself that in an instant she was going to find herself in the presence of this saint, whom in her own thought she was placing far above herself. The devotion of Pouponne toward the old man, who after all, was no real relative of hers, her noble virtues, the charity that she would find ways of practicing in the midst of this abject poverty, the universal respect of which she was the object, everything was overawing Charlotte and she was wondering how she was going to approach this noble Christian woman whose virtues and reputation she envied.

She did not hesitate a moment to enter the house, which was composed of only two rooms. In the better of them had been placed the old man's bed, a few tables and seats of wood, all made by the friends of Pouponne. The other room served as a kitchen and was at the same time the girl's bedroom. A narrow bunk covered with a very clean and very white cotton quilt, a few household utensils and a table with one or two benches composed its furnishings.

At that far-off time, it should be noted, our ancestors had no idea of the luxury that later on their grandchildren were to enjoy. Certainly, among the rich in New Orleans were found some who had sent to Europe for the costly objects destined to decorate their lordly domains; but these were the exceptions, and just as the rich planters were obliged to make on their places all the provisions necessary for their tables, they had to do the same with their furniture which, without exception, was made by the plantation workers. My great-grandfather himself followed this more or less general rule and only used this type of furniture that Charlotte, with her good taste, could make as handsome as it was comfortable. Thus the beds, the armoires, the desks and the tables made of cypress or of walnut (the local woods) were carefully varnished, whereas the chairs, the sofas and the stools were covered with rich camaieu or damask goods, always of brilliant colors and variegated patterns.

One would have said that Pouponne with her innate taste for the beautiful had somehow guessed at the luxury inside these great houses that she had never entered. Her well-rubbed tables shone as if they had been varnished; the rough wood of a settee and of old Landry's armchair was carefully hidden in the folds of light cotton material in a pattern of red squares woven by the nimble fingers of the young Acadian. In addition one found in this modest cabin the luxury of all dwellings, flowers. The children in the area adored Pouponne and contended to gather the most beautiful flowers and take her the largest bouquets of them. Some rather ordinary vases held two bunches of wild flowers: one was placed in Pouponne's room, the other at the head of Landry's bed.

At the moment when the carriage of Madame Bossier was stopping, Pouponne, ever pensive, was knitting socks, seated next to her adopted father, who had just gone to sleep. So deep in thought was the child, that she did not hear the noise of the vehicle. At Charlotte's light knock on the door, she lifted her head and listened, but left her place only upon hearing a second knock. Pouponne had already seen Madame Bossier at church and recognized her when she saw her. As for the latter, she had paid no attention to the

Acadian women and never turned her eyes from her prayer book. Thus, we can say that she was seeing Pouponne for the first time. Face to face with the young girl, Charlotte was looking at her and at the same time in this silent contemplation forgetting what she had to say to her.

Pouponne was twenty, the same age as Charlotte. She was tall and slender, and under a simple dress of violet calico with its fitted bodice the nymph-like contours of her figure stood out with an astonishing grace. For nothing in this world would the young girl have wished to deck herself out in bright colors; though her poverty did not allow her to wear proper mourning for those whom she had left behind and whom in her heart she thought dead, she always wore this mourning in the very depths of her soul. She was never seen participating in the dances and other celebrations; her only visits were those made to the church on Sundays.

Pouponne's face, no matter what Zozo might have said about it, was favored with an almost celestial expression, which moved one to wonder as much as admiration. Seeing her face one could sense sainthood and looked upward in the hope of catching a glimpse of a halo. Although her features had perhaps lost a little of their youthful bloom and her expression some of its old gaiety, Pouponne was still strikingly attractive. As I said, a veil of sadness partially covered the radiance of this beauty. Her big black eyes, always so sad, had kept a sweetness which gave them an inexpressible charm. When she smiled, which rarely happened those days, that smile would brighten her whole appearance and show two rows of beautiful white teeth between coral-red lips. Looking at this child without education, this little *Cadienne*, who had never caught a glimpse of what people call the best circles, one wondered where she had acquired her composed beauty and manners so full of gracious dignity.

Pouponne would have blushed at the thought of going barefoot; it was, she said, a lack of modesty that could only offend God and, poor as she was, found a way to knit stockings. After many tries she also learned to make shoes from alligator hides. *Père* Landry had showed her how to prepare the hides. Her beautiful black hair was always well-combed and gathered in a braid forming a natural crown. This girl's manners had a certain reserve that precluded any undue familiarity and commanded respect, even from Charlotte.

Surprised to see this beautiful woman on the gallery, Pouponne made her finest curtsy and opening the door said: "You want come in M'am?"

Charlotte entered . . . and, must it be said, from the presence of this beautiful girl, from the house's interior that bespoke poverty, one sensed an aura of modesty and cleanliness that stirred in the heart of our visitor an indescribable and uncommon feeling that was winning her heart more and more.

Pouponne offered her a wooden stool; a different person in the presence of this wealthy lady would have blushed and made excuses. Such was not the case with Pouponne; she offered simply the little she possessed and was not in the least embarrassed by her humble living quarters.

"You want sometin', M'am?" she asked when she saw Charlotte comfortably seated.

"Yes. I went out to buy poultry and Madame Labauve, your neighbor, sold me three dozen. She told me that probably you could sell me some too."

"*Mais*, yass," replied the girl, "Zozo, she done tell you de trut', ah got some for sell . . . . You gon' need a big bunch or a lil' bit, M'am?"

Charlotte bit her lip. How could such language come from such a pretty mouth?

"I will buy all you can sell."

"Too bad, dat ain't gon' be much," said Pouponne, "it take some for de bouillon of *père* Landry . . . . Two dozen chicken an' two dozen egg . . . . Dass all ah can do . . . dat enough ma'am?"

"I will have to be satisfied with that. And what is the price, mademoiselle?"

"De same like M'am Labauve."

"Well," said Charlotte, "if you are willing, we will finish this business about the chickens right now, because I have a favor to ask of you."

Pouponne looked at her with amazement, but Charlotte kept talking all the while, taking her purse from her pocket.

"There's two *piastres* for the chickens and one and a half for the eggs; this evening I will send a slave who will help you catch the chickens and will deliver them to me."

"Dass fine, m'am," answered the girl, still very much in her cocoon of cold dignity.

"Now," continued Charlotte, "I have a request. Fr. Jacques talked a great deal to me about you and your father . . . he told me that your father was sick and . . . I took it upon myself to bring him some good things to eat, as is done among neighbors, you know . . . . Furthermore, I am quite anxious to see old Landry . . . may I, Pouponne?"

This name came quite naturally to Charlotte's lips, and the Acadian girl, normally so proud, did not seem offended by this familiarity. She got up and going toward her father's room she said: "Ah axe eem if he want to see you."

A moment later she came back and said: "Come, m'am."

Charlotte had made a sign to her driver, and the latter put down next to her a basket of provisions; she showed it to Pouponne who picked it up without saying a word.

Old Landry was in a semi-upright position on his bed, his shoulders propped up by a pile of very white pillows and his long hands resting on some covers whose cleanliness was a pleasure to see. The fragrance from the bouquet placed near his bed filled the whole room.

Astonished, impelled in spite of herself by a strange fascination and emotionally moved as if she were in the presence of a person of high position, Charlotte, blushing a deep red, advanced toward the old man and, extending her hand, said with respect:

"Good day, *père*!"

"Good day, dear lil' lady" replied the patriarch while pressing the young lady's hands between his own.

"*Père* Landry," said Pouponne while removing from the basket the provisions, which she was arranging on the table, "de lady is our neighbor, a M'am Bossier . . . See de good ting dat she bring you: dem ting dat you not see since long time . . . look deh, look deh . . . good wheat bread, butta', preserve . . . an' . . . oh, *père*, what you want mos' . . . wine!"

The eyes of the old man sparkled with pleasure.

"Oh! tank you! ma good lil' lady; God bless you!"

And turning toward Pouponne: "Ma girl, poh me one glass . . . I gon' drink *santé* to our neighbor."

Pouponne hastened to obey and seeing the old man sip the wine that she had just brought him, Charlotte's heart swelled with joy; she could sense the happiness that her presence had just awakened in this poor house.

In order to have an opportunity to come back, Madame Bossier said nothing about the sewing she intended to offer Pouponne but did obtain from her the promise that she would speak to her every time the old man needed something.

This visit was not the last, and soon a great friendship was established between these two women of such different social and economic backgrounds, but of absolute equality in the practice of virture, both finding but one real pleasure in life, that of alleviating the distress of others. It was through Pouponne's hands that Charlotte channelled her charity. It was Pouponne who would talk to her of the needs of this one, of the sickness of that one; together they visited the cabins of the poor, and soon the name of Madame Bossier was as revered and esteemed as that of Pouponne Thériot.

Charlotte, still so much alone, found great pleasure in this close relationship: thanks to her neighbor, *père* Landry no longer wanted for anything, for if Pouponne refused for herself presents from her new friend, she did accept them for her adopted father. In order to have Pouponne with her for a whole day from time to time, she would send each morning to her cabin an old servant loaded down with food, whose orders were to take care of the laundry and the modest kitchen of her mistress's friends and especially to look after *père* Landry. This new attention from her friend gave a little more leisure to Pouponne, who could now do the sewing for the Bossier family and weave the fine cotton goods that Charlotte would send to New Orleans and for which the merchants always paid premium prices.

X

Fr. Jacques had kept the promise that he had made to Madame Bossier. The Sunday following the one on which he had spoken of the suffering of the Acadians, he related what he knew of the love of Pouponne and Balthazar, and this story increased even more the interest that Charlotte already had in the young girl. I am going to let the reader in on the good priest's story.

"At the time when the troubles were beginning to appear on the horizon, there were living in the village of Grand Pré two well-off families united by all the bonds of friendship begun in childhood. The Landrys and the Thériots were neighbors, and when the elder Thériot died, old Landry proffered his aid and protection to his friend's widow and to the seven children whom he left behind. Madame Thériot would have done nothing, undertaken nothing without consulting her neighbor. The latter was the widower of two wives who had given him twenty children. Like Jacob of holy memory, the old man had bestowed the greater part of his affection on the children of his old age: Norbert, Ursin and Balthazar. The first two, like their elders, were married, and Balthazar, the Benjamin of his old father, of whom he was the idol, alone remained with him.

"On the other side, Pouponne, the only daughter of the widow Thériot, was growing up near her young neighbor and quickly learned to share his affection as she had up to then shared his childhood games.

"To recall in minute detail the origins and phases of his relationship would be futile and impossible. Pouponne and Balthazar began to spin the thread of their love just as their fathers and mothers and brothers and sisters had done before them. They lived one next door to the other; their families were close and their contacts were daily. Balthazar was scarcely four years older than his little neighbor who, at that time, was barely twelve.

"Together they took the religious instructions that I gave them to prepare for the first communion. During several weeks in the company of each other, they followed close to the main road the little path that led to the church. Sometimes Pouponne would trot ahead and sometimes Balthazar would lead in order to smooth the snow or facilitate the passage by muddy ponds; of course, in every awkward situation the stronger sex helped the weaker. Sometimes in order to be more light-footed the two children took off their shoes; then Balthazar would attach the two pairs of shoes by the ends of their laces and hang them from his neck. Then one could see them run about here and there, gay and happy. Balthazar, let us note, paid no attention to Pouponne's little bare feet, which left such pretty imprints as they touched the fresh clay.

"It was one of their customs to take with them their noon snack which they would enjoy on the grass or under the overhang in front of the church. Balthazar liked, among other things, cream cheese or clabbered milk, and Pouponne had a sweet tooth always ready to nibble on a butter cake. Now, it often happened that our little girl's basket contained a tempting cheese resting on fig leaves, whereas Balthazar would remove from his sack a large, well-buttered cake. One need not guess that they shared these things."

The good priest stopped: "Pardon me madame," he said addressing himself to my great-grandmother, "I am letting myself get carried away by my memories and I am relating incidents quite insignificant for you, I am afraid."

"Oh! no," answered the young woman, "everything in your story interests me and while listening to you I like to return to the happy days of my poor Pouponne."

Fr. Jacques continued: "The delights of the snack and all these pleasant neighborly relations did not make the catechism go any the worse. The day of the first communion having arrived, the two children approached the holy table together, and when they returned home to their parents in the midst of the merry-making, a ray of grace shone from their pure and guileless faces. Pouponne was charming under her little white bonnet in her outfit which was as chaste and simple as her soul. A seraph could not have better disguised himself to visit incognito this land of humans.

"As for Balthazar, all his attention was concentrated on a large color print that I had just given to him and which showed a group of chubby angels in flowing garments.

"From that time on Balthazar joined his brothers in the fields, and Pouponne helped her mother in the numerous occupations of a woman in comfortable circumstances. They had learned from their parents the moral vigor which characterized the colonists of that time. Now, within their families they were going to mold themselves into this strong, active, and regular life, into these habits of work, thrift, kindness, and honesty which were the whole secret of the real riches and happiness of the Acadians.

"The mere fact that one finds these two children engaged two years after their first communion proves that their relations progressed beyond the point of clabbered milk and butter cakes. Doubtless, Balthazar no longer saw Pouponne's little white foot, for since they had told the little girl that she was now a big girl, she would have blushed even beneath the sole of this same little foot if she had shown it bare in public. But her foot was not the only delicate thing she had: her face, which at that time, grief had not touched with the dark cloud that veils it today, her pretty little face was so pleasing, so attractive that Balthazar must end by noticing it. Even as they grew up, they did not completely lose the habit of walking together as they went to church or elsewhere. The woods and the fields of the two families adjoined; the men of the families often helped each other during the harvests and often one could see the girls of the families arrive all flushed as they brought dinner to their fathers and brothers.

"After Sunday service they danced sometimes in the flowery meadow in front of the Widow Thériot's house. There were cotillions or rounds danced to a simple air as our poor colonists still dance in this land of exile. In one movement, Balthazar was obliged to cast his scarf around Pouponne's neck; the latter ran away; the scarf was in a slip knot, and in order not to strangle his dancing partner, Balthazar let go. Pouponne ran away toward the house with her fetter which she carefully put away with her white bonnets and little girl trinkets in the bottom of a drawer scented with fragrant herbs.

This scarf, that she kept, was, according to the customs of the area, tantamount to an announcement and became the first bond contracted between these young people in love.

XI

"The next Sunday Pouponne did up her hair to go to church, and this both gave Balthazar great pleasure and did not escape the observant eye of *mère* Theriot. Back at the house at a moment when the two women were alone, the mother said to her daughter:

"'Pouponne, if Balthazar axe you in marriage, wat you gon' say?'

"'Who, me!' cried the child in great astonishment which turned to a smile, 'what I'd say?'

"Then, blushing a deep red, she threw her arms around her mother's neck and with her face hidden on her shoulder, she repeated:

"'What I gon' tell em, well, *chère maman* . . . I'd say . . . yass.'

'An' dat be well said, my chil'!' answered the good woman hugging her daughter; 'Balthazar is a good boy an' I like eem plenty, too.'

"After the great efforts she had just made to expose her secret to two human ears, Pouponne needed a few moments of silence. *Mère* Thériot understood and at the end of a moment, she asked in a voice that was not without a certain tremor:

"'Have you tink of time of marriage, mah lil' girl?'

"'Of course not, *maman*,' replied Pouponne with a little roguish air that fit her well. 'Am I big enough to have a husband? . . . *Mais* by de way, how ol' you was when you take papa?'

"'Fifteen exact.'

"'An' me, I make fifteen in six mont . . . an' if you an' *père* Landry say awright, we make de weddin' December fifteent' . . . dat, you know, is mah birtday.'

"'On mah side, dat fit me like a glove,' replied the mother, 'an' I sure de neighbor gon' tink like me. Six mont'! dat'l give us time for prepare everting for set you up right . . . like prince . . . , nottin' less.'

"A few days after this conversation the parents reached an agreement and I was called into the council. The marriage was set for the fifteenth of December as our little Pouponne had wanted.

"Two months after this engagement, Norbert and Ursin Landry informed their father of their intention of leaving Grand Pré and going to join two of their brothers already established on the banks of the Missaguash at the head of Bay de Beau Bassin. In view of the events which were already under way and of their hatred for the English, the two young Landrys were exiling themselves with their families, leaving their old father sixteen children to help and care for him. The latter preferred to stay in Grand Pré where they had been born and where was everything in the world they possessed. Moreover they still anticipated times of peace and justice, of justice and tranquility under the paternal roof.

"These separations had become increasingly common, but none, perhaps, had been as painful as this one. Norbert and Ursin were, like Balthazar, the favorites of their father; he was old, he could sense the course of events and he would say to himself:

"'My poor boys! will I ever see dem again?'

"He had bought back everything his sons had been obliged to sell: their animals, their furniture; he had kept everything in order to facilitate their trip. In addition he had ordered Balthazar to leave with his brothers to help them in their new home.

"'You come back when dere is no more need for you, he said.'

"They had to leave at night in order to avoid being arrested as traitors. Certainly the departure of his children was cruel for *père* Landry, but, as I have said, his two oldest sons had already settled on the Bay de Beau Bassin and often he received news from them; often they beseeched their father and brothers to come join them. Doubtless, these continually renewed entreaties were the result of just learning of the presence of Monsieur de La Corne, who had just arrived at Beau Bassin with a large group of Acadians. The pleasure of joining their brothers, the increasing obstacles the government was setting up around them, the hope of finding themselves again French . . . all these motives, especially the last, appeared sufficient to Norbert and Ursin to convince them to leave their own country. For the same reasons their father granted them permission to do it.

"Balthazar had gone to get Pouponne in order to enjoy her presence during the few hours he had left in Grand Pré. The brothers and sisters of the Landry boys had gathered around them to help at their departure and to say a last farewell.

"It could have been around eleven at night that old Landry got up, and looking over several groups of weeping women and sleeping children said in a loud voice:

"'My boys, it is time to start out . . . you mus' be far from here at sunup.'

"Then a passage opened up in front of him and in the middle of his sons, daughters, and daughters-in-law, the old man went out first, holding the hand of Norbert's oldest son, aged seven. The conversation in the house had not been at all animated: the voices were trembling, the sentences broken by sobs . . . it stopped completely on the threshold.

"Next to those who were going to leave were lining up those who were going to stay, and all were carrying some kind of burden, some objects of daily usefulness. This procession made its way in silence in the midst of the darkness toward the mouth of the Gaspereau where awaited them the big ship which was going to take away these voluntary exiles. Last in this procession came Pouponne and Balthazar leaning one on the other, their hearts stirred with the darkest forebodings. No stranger, not a friend accompanied the poor emigrants: they were going away like unknown coffins that only relatives accompany.

"They had feared that getting together too big a crowd under old Landry's roof would attract the attention of the authorities, who even in Grand Pré were beginning to keep their ears open. After the arrival on the shore a little more noise was made: the setting up of the women and children and all the household objects in the middle of darkness and the blindness produced by tears created some disorder. They were calling to each other in low voices, preparing the rigging and casting off the moorings. Balthazar was the last to board. He was pressing Pouponne against his chest, covering her tear-filled eyes with kisses and repeating:

"Have courage, my love one! in tree week I be back.'

"Little by little the noise stopped. One could still hear a few voices saying goodbye on different tones of the scale of grief . . . one also heard the cries of children disturbed in their sleep. Poor little ones! a cold and damp breeze was passing over their faces; they felt that it was not the caressing breath of their mothers. A vigorous tossing about began to make itself felt in response to the efforts of the rowers; it was no longer for them the soft rocking of the cradle. They were crying and their voices, rising with the strongly blowing wind, were the last sounds to reach the grandfather's ear from this dark solitude.

"Two persons were the last ones to remain standing on the shore: they were old Landry and Pouponne. When they no longer saw anything of the blurred silhouette on the water, when the waves raised by the oars had stopped taking to the beach the distant and supreme farewell of the travellers, the old man turned toward the child who, though bathed in tears, held her place at his side and said to her with effort in a tremulous voice:

"'Don' cry, mah lil' one . . . you know well dat he come back for de weddin', your Balthazar!'

"Then he passed his wrinkled hand over the young girl's hair, at the same time caressing her cheek and the tip of her pretty little ear. They turned around and with a sigh slowly took the road home. Pouponne walked some time without saying anything, merely bringing the corner of her white apron to her eyes from time to time, but, having arrived at the door of her mother's cottage, she stopped:

"'Ah! *père* Landry,' she cried out, 'sometin' tell me deh, in mah heart, dat ma Balthazar won' never come back.'

XII

It was during two visits that Fr. Jacques told Monsieur and Madame Bossier what I have just written. As he went away, he said to Charlotte:

"Next Sunday I will finish the story of the love of Pouponne and Balthazar."

Indeed, faithful to his promise, he came back and, at Charlotte's insistence, immediately after dinner continued the adventures of the young people at the moment when Balthazar had just left his fiancée.

"Deep in his heart our young suitor nourished the hope of a prompt return, but in spite of this hope the departure was nonetheless painful for him. He had promised his fiancée to return within three weeks and he was determined to keep his promise. As for Pouponne, the departure of her fiancé left her quite sad for four or five days during which her white apron was never free of tears; but as her absent fiancé was supposed to return, she was quickly consoled. Three weeks pass so quickly."

"But instead of three weeks, it was three months that passed without bringing back Balthazar . . . and old Landry grew uneasy as Pouponne wept . . . and the storm that threatened the Acadians grew darker by the day. It was in the course of the fourth month that Balthazar reappeared in Grand Pré the very day of the first proclamation of the English. Without hesitating, without giving his son the time to rest, *père* Landry ordered him to get ready to return to the Bay of Beau Bassin to alert his brothers to the danger that threatened the Acadians. He added to this message the order to abandon immediately the refuge that they had chosen.

"It was a terrible danger to which Balthazar was going to expose himself by leaving Grand Pré at such a time. He knew well that if he was taken, he would probably be shot without any sign of mercy. And yet he did not hesitate . . . Ah! it is because the order of a father has always been a sacred thing for the Acadians.

"Without any remarks the young man got up and began the preparations ordered by his father. Then he went to the Widow Thériot's, told Pouponne of the orders that he had just received and held her to his heart in a last farewell! Since that time not one of us has heard of Balthazar Landry.

"You know the rest of this story; you know how the Acadians, separated on three different ships, were cast ashore on the coasts of New Jersey and Massachusetts. Some, very few, alas! met again. From time to time we see arriving here some of those who remained behind. But my poor Pouponne, with the exception of 'Tit Toine, her younger brother, has never run into any of her own people. She still has hope, however, and I hope with her. God is doubtlessly preparing for her a reward for her resignation and good works. Furthermore, Balthazar did not leave alone; Périchon, one of Pouponne's brothers, accompanied him on his last trip to the Bay of Beau Bassin, and, if one returns, in all probability the other will return with him."

"Thank you!" said Charlotte with emotion while holding Fr. Jacques' hands within her own. "Oh, how I am going to love Pouponne! how I am going to try to make her forget her misfortunes!"

And indeed, as I have said, my great-grandmother did everything to win the friendship and confidence of the young Acadian and let no opportunity pass that could bring them closer. The days that Pouponne came to spend on the plantation were days of happiness for both of them. It was with growing surprise that Charlotte and her husband observed the veritable treasures of intelligence contained in the soul of this child of nature. One would have said that books had opened a new existence for her and had introduced her into unknown worlds where all was a surprise for her. Poor child, who did not know how to read, she found an inexpressible pleasure in listening to people read and paid really remarkable attention to what her friends read her. Nothing astonished her; she understood everything she heard and needed very little explanation. Soon she expressed a desire to learn to read, and, at her insistence, Charlotte gave her her first lessons. At the end of three months, our little *Acadienne* could read as well as her teacher and could soon relieve the loneliness of old Landry with pious and interesting readings.

The poor child never spent a night away from home; how could she abandon her adopted father at night? But, as noted, she came now and then to spend long days with her new friend. For these hours she would leave the old man in the care of old Céleste, faithful and devoted slave to whom Charlotte had given the task of entertaining and caring for *père* Landry during the absences of his daughter. And gradually, without her noticing it, a real revolution was taking place in Pouponne: always in contact with people of refined manners and pure and careful speech, she quickly adopted both. She was determined to learn to write and she succeeded as she had done with reading. In a year, in addition to reading and writing, Charlotte taught her German and all the embroidery known at that far-off time. The income that she received from her sewing and cotton goods allowed the young girl to dress with more elegance. She wore bought shoes and the dresses she made with her exquisite taste were delightfully flattering to her. Those who met her at Madame Bossier's could not fail to notice her beauty, her grace and instinctive elegance, her lovely speech, and charming manners.

She adored reading and consecrated to it all the time she could spare from the work and attention demanded by her old friend's feeble condition. Monsieur Bossier himself chose the books that he lent the girl, and in this manner, while directing her reading, was helping her to acquire the education that was more and more becoming for him an object of continual surprise. The pastor could not get over it and *père* Landry, so proud of the learning of his daughter, while speaking of her, would say:

"How she is educate, our Pouponne! I believe for sho' dat she know right now, jus' as much as de pries'! For sho' she talk dat Latin (German) jus' as good as him!"

We know Pouponne and realize that she never neglected the good she could do others. In gratitude for the knowledge that she owed to her friends, she told herself that her duty dictated that she share it with those who were deprived of it. She informed Charlotte of the project she had conceived of becoming schoolmistress for the children of the settlement. My forebear not only admired, but even more, approved the project, and it was decided that as soon as winter was over, they would add a large room to *père* Landry's cabin, and there, Pouponne could teach the children and care for her old father at the same time.

XIII

About three months after the first visit Charlotte paid Pouponne, an incident occurred that during several days disturbed the peace which reigned in the calm Bossier household.

One morning Fr. Jacques, who was coming with the last sacrament for a sick person in the vicinity, stopped by casually to ask to share his new friend's lunch. He was always welcome on the plantation, and acting as he did, knew he would please Charlotte and her husband.

Scarcely had the young lady taken her place at the table opposite her husband, who was seated between the priest and his younger brother, when they heard outside a formidable noise accompanied by loud voices and veritable broadsides of the coarsest imaginable language. The guests looked at each other . . . terror colored Charlotte's face: she had recognized the voice of Térencine. She looked at Placide . . . the young man was the color of death and he was keeping his eyes lowered.

"What is it, Vulcain?" my great-grandfather asked the servant who was entering at the moment.

"Master," replied the slave, "It's one of the Cajun women from the settlement. She's angry about something and wants to see you."

"Fine!" answered Monsieur Bossier while getting up, "I am going to see what she wants."

And seeing the priest was about to follow him:

"No! no!" he said, "finish your lunch . . . I will be back in a moment."

"No, my son," replied the priest," . . . I can not let you approach this woman all alone . . . she is dreadful. My presence will perhaps impress her: I am going with you."

Hardly had they gone out when Charlotte, pale and shaking all over, turned to her young brother-in-law:

"Oh, Placide!" she cried, "what have you done?"

"Nothing that could stir up this storm," he answered while getting up and making his way to his room, where he locked himself in.

The young man approached the window and noticed Térencine, filthier and more disheveled than ever, gesticulating and shrieking like a madwoman. Charlotte backed up in spite of herself; this woman terrified her.

Monsieur Bossier, accompanied by the priest, went out on the gallery, but he did not go down into the yard; he remained standing on the first step of the stairs, examining Térencine with an astonished look. She was continuing her shouting and gesturing like a person possessed, shaking her fists at the house as if it were an enemy she was calling in her rage.

"Be so kind as to speak lower, madame," said my ancestor with this cool dignity which characterized him; "no one is deaf here."

"Maybe so," she replied, "but you mus' admit at same time you got some damn sly one wid you at you house. Ah jus' say dat."

Before Monsieur Bossier had time to answer such impertinence, Fr. Jacques moved down one step.

"Madame Théogène," he shouted, "what does such language mean and what are you coming here to do?"

"For what ah come do?" she retorted in a still shriller voice, "I come for axe dat man deh wat his no good broder done to de hona' of mah chil'."

Monsieur Bossier showed indignation, but Térencine, without giving him the time to answer, continued:

"Yeah! yeah! cause dat low-down Placide got himsef money an' a mout', cause he educate like a pries' an talk Latin bout as good as him, tink he has right to run over body of po' people an' fool de girl. Ah! he like too much to have good time and ruin evertin', dat puppy . . . I tol' him not to come rub agains' my girl! Where he is, dis tramp? . . . dis highway robba'? Ah want break him in piece . . . cause I warn him I'd stir him up good."

We know that once she was started, it was hard to stop Térencine. In vain did the priest try to raise his voice; that of the shrewish woman prevented anything being heard; in vain did Monsieur Bossier try to impose silence with a gesture; she shouted, stamped her foot and spewed out insult upon insult. Finally, taking advantage of a moment when she stopped from lack of breath, Monsieur Bossier, trying to master his indignation, said to her:

"I don't understand a word of what you say, madame. What did my brother do to your daughter? and what are you coming to look for here?"

It was with barely contained rage and gestures of an enraged she-wolf that Térencine told that Placide had paid several visits to 'Tite Mine, that at the Saturday dances he only danced with her, had given her several lovely presents, had gone so far as to kiss her (*béquer*, she said) and that never, ever had he spoken of marriage.

"I don't see anything bad in all that," said Fr. Jacques, "nothing but a little puppy love like all the young people have."

Térencine became green with rage and with fists on her hips, she advanced toward the priest:

"Ah!" she shouted, "dat's de way you gon' take it! You, de man who talk wit God! you ought be shame to call dat scoundrel's crime a puppy love! . . . Come on, pries', I'm not smart 'bout de business of sweet talk . . . I don't got word in my hand like you for deal it out to every one dat come to confessional! like in church, but what I see, I can say. If you say dese people right, it's cause dey rich, an' cause you come stuff you belly at dey house when de fodder she run out by you."

"That will do!" shouted Monsieur Bossier as he stamped his foot. "Be so kind as to tell me what you want, and above all, make it quick."

Intimidated by the tone and bearing of my great-grandfather, Térencine lowered her voice.

"I done tol' you awready; you broder, dat one dey call Placide, he steal mah daughter's good name . . . mah lil' 'Tit Mine! an' you mus' understan', *missié*, dat only de *sacrement* can fix up such a tear. (After all her ranting and raving she referred to the loss of honor as a scratch, "acorchure [*sic*]".) If Placide refuse to take her for his wife . . . mon Dieu! . . . ah jus' tell you one tin': poor girl! she gon' tire hersef out sometin' terrible to find hersef one husband!"

My ancestor's expression became darker and darker; he was pale and kept his eyes fixed on the ground, while his nervous movements betrayed a violent emotion.

"Madame," he said, lifting his eyes, "I love my brother as if he were my son; I planned a brillant future for him . . . but if you have told me the truth, if he dared abuse the love and confidence of an innocent child, I swear that he will marry her . . . whatever may be for him the consequence of this union!"

"Ah! monsieur! what are you saying?" cried the priest.

"Well! after all" interjected Térencine ready to lunge at the priest's throat "ain't a po' girl as good as a rich boy?"

And turning back to Monsieur Bossier:

"Got to admit you talk some good, *missié*! Got to do de weddin' right now . . . de priest is here, an' I'm gon' fetch 'Tite Mine."

"Not so fast; first of all I have to hear what my brother has to say about your accusations."

"You are right, monsieur," said Fr. Jacques.

Térencine sprang at him: "You want shut you mout', you!" she exploded while threatening him with both fists. "You patch up cassock! wit dat face wit no meat on it so it's a wonda' you alive! Broke down dead body! Ol' match dat won't light! *Mais*, look at eem den. Sure enough he make me wonda'! Ol' skin an' bone! Believe me an' don' mess in mah business, or pries' or not, I show you sometin' not make you laugh!"

Fr. Jacques was speechless before such insolence: Térencine had reeled off her litany of insults with such volubility that it had been impossible to interrupt her.

Without seeking to stop her, Monsieur Bossier called out:

"Vulcain!"

An enormous Negro came from the dining room and appeared on the gallery.

"Vulcain, go cut two good quince branches."

Vulcain went toward the orchard and came back a moment later holding two long and very flexible switches.

"Stay there," his master said to him, "and if that woman dares to raise her voice and say a single word, you will chase her away using your whip."

This time Térencine almost suffocated from suppressed rage, but the sight of the black colossus intimidated her. She held her tongue; but if her eyes had been pistols, the three men would have fallen dead at her feet.

"Father," said Monsieur Bossier, "please stay a few moments more to watch this woman; I don't want her to get away. This business must be settled this very morning. I am going to get my brother."

And, turning toward Térencine, who, silent in spite of herself, was glaring at the quince branches.

"Madame," he said, "be assured that justice will be done to you."

And he made his way to his brother's room. Placide was waiting for him, his head buried in his hands.

XIV

Monsieur Bossier was eight years older than his young brother and had always considered him as a son. He questioned him calmly and tenderly, and Placide, confronted with this kindness, this paternal interest, told everything. He had certainly attached no importance to his relationship with the pretty little Cajun girl, and after all, had done nothing except what he had seen his comrades often do. He was young, high-spirted, liked to have a good time, and had let himself be attracted toward pretty 'Tite Mine by a feeling to which he could certainly not give the name of love. It was he who took her to the dances held every Saturday, and of course, danced with her. On New Year's Day, returning from New Orleans, he had taken her a gold cross and rings, a blouse and a few ribbons. That's all!

His brother listened to him in silence.

"And," he asked, "did you talk to this girl about love?"

Placide hesitated, but his frankness prevailed.

"Yes, brother."

"Then," said the elder brother staring at him, "you love her, then? . . . you want to make her your wife?"

The young French Fleming, raised in the midst of the most refined aristocracy, had his share of ambition. The thought of marrying this little Cajun girl, who did not even know how to read, would never have occurred to him.

"Oh! brother!" he cried with indignation, "I'd rather die!"

"Placide," continued his brother, "swear to me on the memory of our sainted mother, swear to me that you have no base action to reproach yourself with in regard to his child, whom Térencine accuses you of having seduced!"

Before he had even finished this sentence, the younger man raised his hand to a picture of Christ which decorated the room.

"On this image of Christ," he said, "on the memory of the mother whom I have never known, I swear that 'Tite Mine Simoneau is as pure as the day when I saw her for the first time."

"Fine, brother! I believe you!" said the elder, extending his hand to his beloved brother. And Placide, deeply moved, could see through the tears that were dimming his eyes that those of his brother were as wet as his own. They remained a moment without speaking. At the end of this moment Monsieur Bossier raised his head.

"Listen, my friend," he said, "to avoid outrageous scenes like the one that Térencine just created for us, in order not to expose ourselves again to the charms and traps of Mademoiselle 'Tite Mine Simoneau, you will begin your preparations for leaving. Tomorrow you will leave to go finish your studies at the Jesuit College in New Orleans." [Editor's note: An obvious anachronism. The college in question was founded in 1847.]

Placide lowered his head in silence; he understood that his brother was right and the only thing left for him to do was obey.

Monsieur Bossier went down and came to rejoin Fr. Jacques on the gallery; the latter was walking to and fro watching from the corner of his eye Térencine, who, tired by battle, had let herself slump on the last step of the stairs. She had hidden her face between her knees as if to stifle her rage and to avoid the sight of the formidable Vulcain, who to amuse himself was whipping the ground with his quince branches.

Upon noticing his host in the dining room where he had stopped to say a few words to his wife, the pastor walked over to meet him.

"Well?" he asked.

"You were right, Fr. Jacques, it was a simple flirtation, a pastime. But what can we do to get rid of that loud woman?"

"Offer her some money."

They came back together on the gallery that was closely guarded by Vulcain. Térencine had judged it more prudent to contain herself and she bit her lip to restrain the outburst of her rage. On hearing the noise of their steps she sat up straight, just as a Jack-in-the-box springs up when opened, and cried:

"Should I go get 'Tite Mine?"

"No," replied Monsieur Bossier, "nothing dishonorable took place between my brother and your daughter. He refuses to marry her."

"Oh! de good-for-nottin'!" she shouted, forgetting about Vulcain in her anger. "He don't want marry her, from what you say? Well! we see . . . ah make a string bean out de body of dat good time boy . . . get his deat' notice ready . . . I'll jus' say dat! His daddy was robber, but he don' want marry a decent girl!"

"Vulcain!" called my ancestor.

The Negro advanced completely ready to carry out the orders of his master.

"Oh! dat awful darky!" cried Térencine backing up. "Don't touch me! or I find way turn you white by turn you skin inside out."

"Madame Théogène," said my great-grandfather with this noble dignity that impressed everyone, even Térencine, "how much do you estimate the honor of your daughter is worth? I am disposed to pay for it."

"Money!" she cried, "it's money you want give me! yes, it's like dat wit' rich people . . . . Dem, dey ruin a poor girl, dey do a hundred t'ousand' bad ting an' dey clean it wit' money . . . . Ah! *missié*! you not know Térencine yet.
I want de sacrament of marriage . . . nottin' but dat."

"Listen," continued Monsieur Bossier, "for the last time I am asking you how much money you want . . . otherwise you will have nothing and Vulcain will accompany you to the yard gate; and careful! if ever again you dare set foot in here."

She appeared to be reflecting. Raising her head:

"Well den, twenty *gourdes* (dollars)," she said.

My great-grandfather pulled from his pocket a long bag filled with gold and withdrew from it several quadruples.

"There's a hundred," he said, "and now leave . . . above all, don't come back to bother us."

The eyes of the virago took on a wild look at the sight of all that gold; she was holding her hand open, devouring the gold pieces with her greedy stare.

"But," she said, "if Placide come run behin' ma lil' girl, what we gon' do?"

"Don't worry, tomorrow my brother will leave for college."

It is to be presumed that Térencine regretted this departure. She was already hoping that another visit from Placide would be worth some more gold coins; and certainly she was not beyond inviting him.

As it had been anticipated, Placide left the following day for the Jesuit college, recently established in New Orleans. Charlotte wept on seeing her young brother-in-law go away; she was losing a cheerful companion, always so kind and considerate to the one whom he called his sister. But, deep down inside, the young woman approved her husband's decision.

XV

Charlotte remained sad several days after Placide's departure; it was he who kept her company during the hours her husband spent in the fields. He was so likeable! so high-spirited! he would read to her and always had some amusing anecdote to tell. And what made the solitude of the young woman sadder was that Pouponne no longer came to see her. What did that mean? She would have gone herself to get information at her friend's cabin, but one of her little girls was suffering from a slight sore throat, and she could not think for a moment of leaving the child.

What kept Pouponne at home was the declining strength of her adopted father. He was not sicker, but like a lamp burning down when the oil is exhausted, the life of the old man, worn out by age, was threatening to flicker out.

Sometimes on Sunday after Mass Fr. Jacques would send 'Tit Toine to spend the day with his sister; and it was a great joy for Pouponne to see her dear, little brother coming. He was all the family she had left.

It was the tenth of September. A terrible storm was raging outside and causing the frail cabin to shake. Pouponne, seated beside the old man's bed, was listening to the rain falling in torrents and the fearsome noise of the thunder, which made her tremble in spite of herself. More than once she brought her hand to her eyes to avoid being blinded by the lightning, which from time to time flashed through the sky. It was Sunday, and Fr. Jacques had allowed 'Tit Toine to eat dinner with his sister. The boy was seated on the floor near the fire he was fixing, for although winter was still far-off, fire was already needed by the old man whose blood was chilling in his veins. Suddenly, *père* Landry raised his head:

"Pouponne!" he called.

"I am here next to you, my father," answered his adopted daughter, "do you want something?"

"We are in Septemba', ain't we?"

"Yes, father, today is the tenth."

"De tent'," he repeated, "de tent' of Septemba'! jus' six year go since de moment when we leave Acadie! Maybe de good Lord pick dis day to see me die?"

"Come now!" answered Pouponne while trying to smile, "chase those bad ideas away, *père*. Don't talk about dying . . . . You know you can't leave me before the return of Balthazar!"

A sigh was the only answer from *père* Landry.

"Do you want me to read you something, *père*?" she asked at the end of a moment.

"Yes," he answered, "read me de Prayer for de Dyin'."

"What an idea!" cried Pouponne, "no, that would make you too sad . . . . Hold on, I have something here quite interesting, something Monsieur Bossier himself recommended for me to read: it's about the discovery of America. You know very well that you like stories of trips and battles . . . . You want me to begin?"

"No," he said, "not before I listen to de Prayer for de Dyin'."

It was necessary to yield to his wishes. The young girl, who had gotten up to get the travel book in her room, brought back instead her prayer book and knelt next to his bed. 'Tit Toine got up.

"Sister," he said, "I'm gon' do de secon' part. Litanies--dey know me--I learn dem wit de pries'."

And, for several minutes, one heard in this poor room only the noise of the rain and the wind and the voice of the girl to which was blended her brother's. The old man repeated the responses after the boy.

When Pouponne got up, *père* Landry called 'Tit Toine:

"Lil' one," he asked, "you rememba' you mama?"

The boy was very intelligent for his age; he looked at the old man attentively with his big eyes like his sister's.

"Oh! *père* Landry," he replied, "can a boy forget his mama?"

"But you was so lil' when you leave her!"

"I was six."

"And today you are twelve. An' you twin, lil' one? how you lose him?"

"I not lose him, *père* Landry; de good Lord take him . . . . Poor 'Tit Tienne, he always sick . . . an' he call for his *maman* which make all de people cry on de big ship. And Pouponne an' de mama, dey not dere for take care of him.

I do all I can, but what six year ol' boy can do? I take evertin' good people give me eat . . . . It not much, but all de same, it was sometin'. One night jus' like dat he tell me: 'Tit Toine, I hear *maman* . . . she call me. Goodbye broder!' den he was dead! an' I got no more twin!"

The child stopped choked by the tears . . . but at the moment when Pouponne drew him to herself to console him, he straightened up.

"An' dat's not all!" he cried, his eyes wide-open as if riveted on a frightful sight," . . . de wors' part, here it is! I hol' de body of my twin in my arm an' I try heat his po' col' han', when some bad soldier came grab him 'way from me . . . an' . . . oh! *père* Landry! oh! Pouponne! you know what dey do to my *cher* 'Tit Tienne? Dey trow him in de water!"

Pouponne, who was sobbing as he was, her elbow on the edge of the bed, threw her arms around her brother's neck, pulled him up on his knees and supporting him said:

"'Tit Toine, we must love each other as we did when there were seven of us."

"'Tit Toine," went on *père* Landry, "you got sometin' you want say to you mother and to you twin?"

"What you mean, *père*?" asked the little boy as he looked at the old man in astonishment.

"Jus' dis, my boy: before tomorrow, I be up dere wit' friends an' de good Lord alone know who dey gon' be I'm gon' find again up dere in heaven."

"Don't talk like that, *père* Landry," said Pouponne, "you are not sicker and you still have long days ahead, thank God!"

He shook his head silently. The storm continued with increasing fury; the rain, falling in torrents on the walls of the cabin, was threatening to take off its flimsy roof. From time to time a brilliant flash of lightning crossed the room and was followed by a thunderclap which made the sick man shudder and brought forth cries of terror from 'Tit Toine who had come to take his place again near the fire. There was something which inspired a profound sadness in listening to the unleashing of the elements and the muted groans of the old man struggling against death itself.

"Oh!" Pouponne was saying to herself, "if I could notify Charlotte! ask her for help! but, would it be too cruel to make this child go out in such weather?"

"'Tit Toine!" suddenly said the dying man.

The child hurried to the bed.

"Where is de pries'?"

"I left him dis morning at his house."

"Den, he not eat at de big house?"

"No, *père*."

Pouponne, in desolation, was noting all the indications of death on the features of her old friend. His pallor was becoming cadaverous; two big bluish circles were surrounding his already half-dimmed eyes, and now and then a strange chill ran over his whole body.

"Pouponne!" he called, "Pouponne! I want see de pries'!"

How can you refuse a dying man the last favor he asks? How can you speak of the dangers of a storm to someone who has, perhaps, only a few hours to live? She did not hesitate.

"'Tit Toine," she said, "get up! you have to get Fr. Jacques."

"Listen to de t'under, sister," said the already completely frightened child.

"You have to," repeated Pouponne. "*Père* Landry is very sick and he doesn't want to die without receiving the last sacraments. I'd go myself to spare you this ugly job, but I can't leave this poor old man at such a time."

And all the while speaking, the courageous girl was bundling up her brother in her thickest shawl, attaching his hat on his head with a wool scarf and, putting an umbrella in his hand:

"Listen to me carefully: first you will go to the Labauves' cabin and you will ask Zozo, for me, to let Baptiste go with you. The umbrella is big enough for both of you. Above all hurry, little brother, remember that death does not wait; repeat carefully to the priest that *père* Landry is dying and is asking to see him."

And hugging her brother, after commending him to the Virgin Mary, she opened the door for him while repeating:

"Above all, little brother, hurry!"

She came back to sit near the bed, and although it was barely four o'clock, the darkness was such that she found herself obliged to light a candle. And in the middle of the silence the voice of the dying man would rise from time to time, sometimes to relate some scene of his youth, sometimes to speak of his lost birthplace, or to call the beloved one who had gone before him to the tomb and those whose fate was unknown to him. And he would stop to pray, or fall into a sleep that more than once Pouponne mistook for death.

XVI

We are now going to leave Pouponne right in the middle of her sad and lonely vigil in order to follow 'Tit Toine on the journey he had just begun. As his sister had ordered him to do, he stopped at the Labauve cabin and delivered to Zozo the message from Pouponne. In any other circumstance, the mother would have perhaps refused to expose her child to the danger of that kind of storm, but it was a question of a dying person, and among Acadians an almost limitless respect is shown to those who are going to die. And, according to them, to refuse them something would call down heaven's curse on the head of the one who would dare to commit such a crime. Before Zozo had the time to answer 'Tit Toine, the old grandmother spoke out:

"He got to go, my daughter; who know, maybe it come my turn tomorrow."

Zozo did for her son what Pouponne had done for her brother: she wrapped him up the best she could . . . put his father's blanket-overcoat over his clothes and put in his hands his grandmother's staff.

"Dat's in case you run into sometin' bad," she said.

In a moment, one could see our two little boys close together, there two heads under the umbrella, and making their way as fast as possible toward the priest's house six miles away. It was a long trip for these two children, and they were telling each other that night would certainly overtake them before they had time to reach the rectory. About the middle of the trip was a little wood about a half-mile long, and it goes without saying that getting through this wood was a vivid terror for our little travelers.

"Good Lord," Baptiste was saying, "ain't it too hard on de livin' to have folks die at night an' wit dis kin' weather? As if *père* Landry can't put off to die 'til tomorrow?"

"Yes," said 'Tit Toine, who in his capacity of altar boy, thought himself quite well up on religious matters, "it's really true dat de weather is good for dog, but not for Christian. *Mais*, don't you see, Baptiste, dis poor man, he might have a big sin on his soul an' he want rattle it off to de pries' before he give up his soul . . . ."

At that moment a violent thunderclap was heard and the two boys uttered a cry and clung even closer together.

"If we had jus' take a *jabloroc*," observed 'Tit Toine.

What the child called *jabloroc* was what we call a lantern, and you must admit it would scarcely have been a luxury in the midst of the darkness which surrounded them.

"Dog-gone!" interjected Baptiste, "you got to admit it make dark like de devil here tonight . . . dese woods look to me like about as long as a day without food . . . an' dey mus' be full to de top wit' robber."

"An' maybe some wolf, too!" said 'Tit Toine, who in trying to reassure himself, was making an attempt to be brave at the expense of his comrade. "Ah! what a blessin' de good Lord share wit us when he left all de wolf far away in Acadie!"

"But de robber," repeated Baptiste.

"You want me to tell you de real trut', Baptiste?" continued Pouponne's brother, "you talk like a coward, an' you are one, too. Dere you are! what you tink dey gon' steal from us?"

"Oh! well, you umbrel' . . . an' worse dan dat . . . my stick."

"Well, you jabber too much my lil' man," said 'Tit Toine with a sort of scorn. "It's pretty late an' I'm pretty well tire out . . . it seem my eyes are full of needle prick . . . besides, I'm not do anytin' but stagger round in de dark! I'm sleepin' while I'm walkin' . . . so I'm gon' stop a bit . . . what you tink about dat, Baptiste?"

"I tink dat fit me like de bridle fits de pries' mare," answered Zozo's son while stretching out on the wet grass next to his comrade.

They had been there about two minutes at the very most when they heard someone walking close by, and a voice distinctly said:

"I believe we are lost for sure."

In an instant our two little boys were on their feet and hand in hand were getting ready to flee, when a big hand fell on Baptiste's shoulder and a voice uttered a single word: "Halt!"

Without understanding the meaning of the word, they stopped, and in the light of the lantern carried by the one who had spoken, they noticed two men dressed in uniforms, or rather in remnants of uniforms. One was very tall and broad-shouldered, while the other one, younger in appearance, was both shorter and thinner. Both had their faces covered by thick beards.

"Where are you two going in such weather, little people?" asked the elder of the two men.

It was 'Tit Toine who answered; Baptiste's teeth were beating like a drum, as our altar boy later told his sister.

"We are going to get Fr. Jacques for a po' ol' man who is gon' die."

"Fr. Jacques!" repeated the stranger.

"Or, well, de parish pries', it's all de same," said 'Tit Toine.

"Then, you must hurry, my children," continued the stranger, "Death does not wait. We, too, need to see the priest; we will go with you. Do you still have far to go?"

"Oh no! We are on de way for at leas' two hour. We arrive very soon," said 'Tit Toine while getting under way and holding Baptist even tighter.

Neither of our little boys was too pleased with the company so unceremoniously thrust upon them. The younger of the strangers had said nothing; he seemed immersed in his thoughts. On several occasions they noticed him raise the lantern he held to examine better the features of 'Tit Toine.

Soon our travelers emerged from the woods and noticed in the distance several lights, which certainly had to come from some dwelling.

"Dere it is," said 'Tit Toine, "it's Fr. Jacques' house."

This house, or rather the rectory, was rather large, though as crudely built as all the Acadian dwellings. There were two rooms in front: one was the bedroom of the priest, the other the one where he took his meals, wrote his sermons and received those who came to see him and consult him. In the rear there were two other rooms: the largest and best furnished was called the guest room, and there was always a bed ready for the friend or the unfortunate person who came to ask Fr. Jacques' hospitality. In the last one slept old Pélagie and 'Tit Toine. At that time, from fear of fire no doubt, the kitchens were always kept at a distance from the principal lodging; Fr. Jacques' was about fifty feet from the house.

'Tit Toine, who felt quite at home in the rectory and knew every corner of it, showed the strangers into what was called the priest's study.

"Wait dere," he told them, "I go tell pries' you here."

The two men sat down in silence; they appeared deeply moved.

'Tit Toine, accompanied by Baptiste, entered the room of the priest, who although it was only seven o'clock, was getting ready to go to bed.

"Good Lord!" he exclaimed upon seeing his altar boy appear, "'Tit Toine" and in such a storm! Why didn't your sister keep you with her? and how do you happen to have Baptiste with you?"

'Tit Toine told Fr. Jacques the object of his mission and ended on these words:

"Pouponne, she say you mus' hurry."

"All right," said the priest, "go hitch up the rig while I get dressed. It is not necessary for you to go with me. Keep Baptiste with you until tomorrow and tell Pelagie to give you some supper."

"Yes, Father."

And at the moment the priest was going to leave, 'Tit Toine turned back:

"Oh! Father," he said, "I foget to tell you dat in you office dere are two men we meet in de wood . . . an' dey follow us 'til here, an' dey want to see you. From what it look like, dey have sometin' tell you."

"Strangers! in this storm! and at this hour! what can they want ask of me? hospitality, no doubt."

He entered the room where the two men were waiting for him. They got up and greeted him respectfully when he appeared. The priest looked at them and a strange emotion took possession of his whole being.

"You wish to see me, gentlemen?"

"Yes," answered the elder of the strangers who could not have been more than twenty-five.

"That voice" . . . said Fr. Jacques, "those eyes" . . . Oh! I am not mistaken . . . . It's Balthazar."

And he held out his arms to the young man.

After they had clasped each other in their arms for a moment, the pastor turned toward Balthazar's companion and looked at him attentively:

"And that one?" he asked.

"That one," answered the young man as he moved closer, "is Périchon . . . didn't you recognize him?"

"No," replied Fr. Jacques, "that beard disguises you too well."

At that moment the two younger boys were coming back in. At the name of Périchon, 'Tit Toine gave a cry.

"Périchon!" he said, "I remember dat before in de ol' place I had a brother who was call like dat."

"And it's really your brother who is there, 'Tit Toine," said the young Acadian while picking up the boy in his arms. "Ah! little brother! we are the only two left now."

'Tit Toine was going to cry out again and speak of Pouponne, but on a sign from the priest, he kept silent.

"Balthazar, this is not the time to tell each other what happened on both sides since our separation; later we will question each other. These two children have come on foot in the middle of the night and in the storm to get me to take the last sacraments to a dying man. Do you know who the dying man is, Balthazar?"

"I am afraid to guess," answered the young man, "it's my father."

"My rig is ready," continued the priest, "let's hurry, my son . . . . God grant that your father not die without having seen you again . . . without having blessed you. Perichon, you will stay here tonight and tomorrow 'Tit Toine and

Baptiste will take you to the cabin where *père* Landry lives with his daughter."

"His daughter!" repeated Balthazar, "which one?"

Père Jacques pretended not to hear and addressed himself to 'Tit Toine:

"When we have left," he said, "you can tell your brother all that you know of your family. Tell him all, my boy."

And while Balthazar, seated in the *calèche* next to the priest, was making his way to the cabin where his father was dying, 'Tit Toine was talking of Pouponne and Périchon, and wishing to obey his pastor to the letter, was telling him all the news of the settlement.

"On arriving you must not identify yourself," said the priest to Balthazar, "the joy would kill your father before he has had the time to prepare himself for death. Let me take care of things: when it's the right time, I will give you a sign."

Too moved, too sad to talk, Balthazar nodded assent. He felt happy to see his father again, to be able to embrace his sister . . . but at the same time his heart was breaking at the cruel thought that it was to see him die that he was going to be reunited with his father.

XVII

The *calèche* stopped in front of the cabin. They got out: followed by Balthazar, Fr. Jacques carrying a little bag for the viaticum entered the room which served as bedroom and kitchen for Pouponne. This room had certainly changed in appearance since the first time Charlotte entered it. Pouponne was proud, we know, and refused all the gifts that her friend tried to give her, but she felt more ill at ease with Monsieur Bossier and did not dare show her pride too openly in his presence.

Often without attaching too much importance to it, she had told Charlotte how displeasing it was to do the cooking in the room where she slept, and one day while she was eating at the plantation, Monsieur Bossier sent his carpenter with his helpers to *père* Landry's, and when she got home in the evening Pouponne found a little kitchen, which pursuant to the orders of the plantation owner, had been built a short distance from the cabin.

The gift was a little too heavy to be returned, and Pouponne had no choice but to thank those who had so thoughtfully done her a favor.

And now that the room was cleared of its kettles, buckets and other utensils of this type, Pouponne found the means to transform it into a charming little nest that Balthazar observed with increasing surprise. Next to the girl's little white bed was a *prie-dieu* covered in brilliant colors. Over it hung an image of Jesus on the cross that Pouponne herself had framed. Shelves decorated with books could be seen on the walls. The chairs, like the *prie-dieu*, were covered with bright-hued materials. Here and there one saw charming baskets woven by the agile fingers of Pouponne and which contained the most beautiful flowers of the season. The spinning wheel had kept its place, for our little worker always used it, but on a little table covered with an embroidered cloth, one saw an elegant sewing basket lined with blue satin: it was Placide who had sent it to his sister's friend, and this basket was filled with little balls of wool of all colors and a beautiful half-finished tapestry.

Balthazar was examining everything and couldn't get over it . . . . Who then was this woman who was surrounding herself with books, embroideries and flowers? Certainly, it could not have been one of his sisters, for if *père* Landry's daughters were good housekeepers, they were of the type of Zozo and Titine and would prefer a beet to the prettiest flower. Not for a moment did the thought of Pouponne come to Balthazar's mind. He was there in this little room filled with the fragrance of this unknown woman, and his elbow on his knee and face covered by his hand was listening to the sounds coming from the adjoining room where the dying man had just received communion, and where at that very moment the priest was administering the last anointing. The rites finished, the priest said:

"*Père* Landry, there is in the next room a traveler whom I ran into and who followed me here. The storm is still raging . . . can you show him hospitality?"

"Certainly," answered Pouponne, "and since he is in my room, let him stay there. I will take him some supper in a little while."

"No, no, he doesn't need anything," said Fr. Jacques, "he ate at the Leblanc's cabin. But since it's damp and there is no fire in your room, Pouponne . . . can I have him come in here?"

"Why . . . yes," she answered with a little hesitation.

The priest continued: "This traveler told me that he had served in Monsieur de Boishébert's corps . . . who knows! he might be able to give you some news."

The poor octogenarian remained silent a moment taken by a painful trembling which seemed shared by the one who held him up, one arm passed under his venerable head.

Balthazar had come in, and too full of emotion to greet them, had sat near the chimney with his back carefully turned toward those who were in the room.

"Are you an American, sir?" asked *père* Landry in a weak voice.

"No sir, I am an Acadian," replied the young man without turning around.

"Ah! . . . An' it make long time dat you leave Acadie?"

"Nearly a year."

Often *père* Landry had said to himself and had told Pouponne that if Balthazar were alive, he would be in the army . . . now his heart was pounding at the thought that perhaps this stranger had run into his son and could give him some news about him.

"You was belong to Major Boishébert's corps," he said . . . at leas' dat's what de pries' jus' tell me."

"Yes sir, I was under his orders."

"An' tell me," continued the old man with an emotion that was painful to see, "in de army did you ever come 'cross a certain Balthazar? . . . Ah! it's 'cause you see he was my son!"

"Do you mean Captain Balthazar Landry?" asked the young soldier who was making a preternatural effort to control his emotion and did not dare raise his head for fear of giving himself away.

"He wasn't captain dat I know 'bout, but his name was Balthazar Landry from de village of Grand Pré," said the old man, who seemed to have recovered his strength in order to be able to speak of his son.

"Sure I knew him . . . I told you . . . he was my captain."

"Your captain!" cried *père* Landry stupefied.

And tears appeared on his half-closed eyelids, while Pouponne sobbed. The priest, seated at the foot of the bed, was crying like a baby. *Père* Landry looked at them one after the other, and fixing his eyes on the stranger:

"Ah! I understan' all!" he said . . . "I see Fr. Jacques cry . . . my lil' girl, she cry too . . . you, you turn your head from us . . . I know well dat very few return from de war . . . You was his comrade? I guess he sent you tell his papa how he die! . . . Come, my daughter," he added while passing his wrinkled hand over Pouponne's hair, "don't cry like dat . . . you know we was expect his deat' . . . see how calm I am, an' I was his papa!"

"But sir'" said Balthazar without changing position, "my captain is not dead."

A chorus answered him: "Not dead!" cried the old man and the girl at the same time.

For a moment something unexplainable had been going on inside Pouponne; her eyes did not leave the stranger, and her body leaning forward and her ears straining, she was listening to the accents of this voice, which, without realizing it, was causing an undefined uneasiness in her heart. Not for a moment did she suspect the truth, but at the last words of the young man, she got up suddenly leaving the dying man's bed and took a step in the direction of the stranger, joining her hands and looking at him with a pleading and heart-broken expression, as if to say to him:

"In the name of God! speak to us about him!"

Balthazar upon noticing this face which was now bathed in the full light of the fireplace, sat bolt upright on his chair, but feeling at that very instant the hand of the priest on his shoulder, he remained there overwhelmed by his happiness! . . . It was Pouponne, Pouponne whom he was finding near his father! But he had to remain quiet, stifle the emotional outburst from the heart; the life of his father depended on his silence. He could only pronounce the name of Pouponne in his heart.

But Fr. Jacques had forgotten the power of love in the heart of a woman. Pouponne did not keep at a distance . . . instead she took a couple of steps forward and forcibly taking in her own the hands with which the stranger was covering his face:

"Balthazar!" she cried.

Any mystery was useless now. Pouponne rushed into the arms of her beloved and half-fainting yielded to his caresses and embraces. *Père* Landry had not heard the exclamation of the girl, but seeing the lovers in each others' arms, he guessed the truth and raised his trembling hands toward the child who was returning:

"Balthazar! my son!" he cried.

And after hugging his son on his breast:

"I can die now, I have seen him again! an' he will watch over Pouponne."

Questions followed each other without interruption. Pouponne wanted to know if her mother was still alive and where her brothers were, whereas the poor man still found the strength to beg Balthazar to talk to him about his sons and daughters whom he had left behind him.

"Prepare yourself to hear a sad story," said the young man, "I am going to begin at the moment when I left Grand Pré to go take my father's orders to my four brothers."

"Did they obey me?" asked the old man.

"They couldn't; the families of Sosthène and Martin had about fifty members and those of Norbert and Martin about twenty. It takes money for so many people to travel. They therefore stayed at Beau Bassin and did very well. They are still there today, and all are rich and happy."

"Alleluia!" said the old man piously making the sign of the cross.

"That takes care of four of your sons," continued Balthazar; "the fifth is next to you. I learned about the death of Théodule and Onésiphore; as for the others, I have never heard talk of them. As for your daughters; Modeste, Séraphine and Arthémise are dead; Cidalise and Adèle have gone to rejoin their brothers in Beau Bassin. That's all I know about our family."

"And my mother?" said Pouponne weakly.

"Pouponne," said Balthazar, "you must remember that Périchon left with me."

"I remember."

"We never left each other," continued the young man, "we left together, we came back together."

"And where is he?" cried Pouponne.

"At my house, my child," said the priest, "you will see him tomorrow."

"Thank you, God!" exclaimed the poor girl.

XVIII

"It is six years today," said Balthazar picking up his story, "that I returned with Périchon from our trip to Beau Bassin. We arrived at Grand Pré a few hours after the departure of the ships that were taking our families away. It was nighttime: we wandered about the village streets filled with English soldiers. Our anger was terrible, and I believe that I would have become a murderer if one of those monsters had talked to me. I was trying to get into my father's house: it was filled with soldiers who were drinking and singing inside those blessed walls where I had been born, where I had been so happy.

"Périchon, for his part, wanted to go into his mother's house: we had not eaten anything since morning and we were hoping to find some provisions there. We had no trouble slipping in, all the doors and windows were open. We entered and at the moment when Périchon was lighting a candle he had found above the chimney, my feet got caught up in something which was stretched out on the floor. I called Périchon . . . and . . . horror! oh! Pouponne, it was the body of your mother that we had in front of us . . . your dead mother, lying in her blood! . . . Your mother assassinated by the English!"

He stopped: he lacked the strength to continue; Pouponne cried out and a heart-rending sob escaped from her lips.

"Horror!" cried the dying man, "oh! dem monster dat kill women an' chirren!"

Fr. Jacques raised the crucifix and exposed it to the view of the old man.

"The one who died for us on the cross orders us to forgive injuries," he said.

And turning toward Balthazar:

"Continue, my son."

"How did the body of Madame Thériot happen to be there?" continued the young man, "I never found out. Here is what I presume: after seeing her daughter and small children snatched from her, the poor woman must have lost consciousness, and stretched out on the ground she escaped the eyes of those who were watching over the loading of the ships with their human cargo. When she recovered consciousness, she had certainly lost her reason, and she mechanically took the road toward her house. Either to be done with her, or possibly because in her despair she had insulted the English, one of the soldiers ran her through with a saber and left her alone, still living perhaps. When we entered the house, she had been dead for several hours."

"Curse dem! dey who treat a weak woman like dat," repeated the old man.

For the second time the priest raised the crucifix.

Her head leaning on the shoulder of her fiancé, Pouponne, the poor child, was crying all the tears that burdened her heart. Balthazar tenderly kissed her hair and resumed his sad narration.

"A painful but a sacred duty remained for us to perform; we had to take the body of the dear martyr to the cemetery where her husband and eight of her children rested in peace. The bloodied body had to be buried at any risk or price. Perichon kneeling next to his mother seemed to have forgotten everything in his despair. It was only with difficult that I made him understand what we had to do. It is probable that like the other women *mère* Thériot had packed all her personal effects, for we found nothing at first: the armoires, the chests of drawers were open, but they were empty. But then glancing in the direction of his mother's bed, Périchon gave a start: this bed seemed to have been prepared for the night, and it is this circumstance that made me suspect that the poor woman, after the departure of the ships, had returned home and without knowing what she was doing prepared what was needed for the night.

"Périchon removed one of the sheets and lovingly enveloped the body of his mother while I started to look for the shovels we needed. When I re-entered the room Périchon showed me a belt full of gold that he had found on his mother's body under her clothes. It was the poor woman's savings that she had wanted to take away with her in exile."

"'Take this gold Balthazar, said Périchon, it belongs to both of us . . . you are stronger, you will be able to protect it better.'"

"Night was closing in on us and we did not have a minute to lose. We knew that if we were taken we would be shot immediately; but what difference did that make? We had to finish our task at any cost. Fortunately for us the cemetery was not too far away, and situated as it is on a hill, it was doubtful that any soldier would go up to it at night.

"Périchon picked up his mother's body, I followed him with two shovels, and in about half an hour *mère* Thériot was sleeping between her husband and her children."

"Thank you, Balthazar!" said Pouponne in a voice choked with sobs.

He leaned toward her and with kisses covered her grief-stricken face, half-hidden on his shoulder.

"One thing remained for us to do: find General Levis' army. Luckily we had some money, and we did it without too much difficulty. We were both enrolled in the regiment of Monsieur Boishébert."

"Oh Balthazar!" said Pouponne with an entreating grace, "tell our father what you did in the army . . . . Poor dear old man! He is convinced that his son must have accomplished courageous acts, great military exploits . . . and I . . . ah! I think a little like he does! Speak, speak, it will be so good to hear you! . . . that is going to cure him, make him young again!"

And Balthazar in his manly voice began the story of the battle of Condiac and the burning of the rectory in Grand Pré. The old man while listening could not prevent himself from crying out in the outpouring of a somber joy:

"Ah! dat's good, my boy, dose blow you strike dere, you see, dat make you father's old age more easy."

Deep in his heart *père* Landry had always nurtured a profound hatred against the English; this hatred had not grown cold with age, quite the contrary. His recent misfortunes had embittered him and were leaving his soul filled with ill will. He could not tire of listening to this son, who had so well inherited his love of country. While listening to him an unusual vigor took possession of the old man's limbs; his face brightened, an exaltation long missing rekindled the spark of life in his whole being. Every symptom of decline was disappearing from his face! He now sat up straight on his bed. Like Lazarus coming out the tomb at the voice of his divine Master, he was coming back to life at the voice of enthusiasm and patriotism. It was a real miracle that was taking place.

Fr. Jacques was enjoying the change that the son's narration was effecting in the dying man. Balthazar himself was yielding to the charm that his words were producing, and his voice resonated in its most appealing tones. His speech which was only the depiction of what he had seen, the echo of what he had heard, was developing with the power of the action itself in the eyes of his listeners. This natural and incisive eloquence of the soldier, this stirring passion of the patriot devoted to the point of heroism, made an orator of Balthazar in every sense of the word. Thus, when he came to tell of the battle of Sainte Foye where he had earned his captain's epaulettes, Pouponne herself, carried away by enthusiasm, threw her arms around his neck and said:

"Oh! my Balthazar! I am so proud of you!"

"After? . . . my son, after?" interrupted the old man.

"Alas!" continued the young man, "what I have left to say is very sad . . . . One would have said that heaven which had made Périchon my companion had decreed that we would never be separated: after my promotion to the rank of captain, he was made sergeant in my company, and we had the luck to fight always side by side. And, after three years spent together in the army, we were taken prisoner at the same time and thrown on the same prison ship where we stayed locked up for two years."

"Good Lord!" exclaimed Pouponne.

"I will tell you nothing," continued the young officer, "of the cruelty with which we were treated, nor of the privations which were imposed on us. I will tell you only of one incident that occurred during our captivity: there were among the prisoners an old officer, who to pass the time got the idea to teach reading and writing to poor devils like me who had never received any education. Our guards didn't oppose him, but they didn't help him in any way. It was on pieces of old newspapers, on bulletins, on the prayer book that he always carried on his person that this good old soul taught us to read, and thanks to him, when we left the prison ship we could read and write passably well."

"It's one fine ting to be educate," observed the old man, "an' at least Pouponne gon' have a husband who know as much as she do."

XIX

"At the end of two years," resumed Balthazar, "we were let go, and we told ourselves that we had to set out in search of what was left of our families. It was a hard task, for the English had stripped us of the remainder of the five hundred crowns from *mère* Theriot; but we had a good dose of courage, and sometimes on foot, sometimes on some cart when people gave us a ride through charity, we arrived in New York. It was in this city that we found some signs of what we were looking for. While wandering the streets, we found ourselves in front of the posters that Louis Comeau, that brave soul, had posted on the walls of New York as well as those of Boston, Philadelphia, and the other big cities of the English colonies. You know, I suppose, that to guide our unlucky brothers in their search, Comeau, hero that he is, continually sends agents with lists of names that they post everywhere. On the one that was in front of me I read in the midst of about a hundred names that the Landrys and Thériots were in Louisiana on the banks of the Mississippi. They had to be ours, and we had to rejoin them. That's what we were telling ourselves, Périchon and I, and we bravely set out. God alone can tell you the obstacles, the hindrances we ran into. Often we had to stop on a farm for a few weeks to work in order to earn the wherewithal to continue our trip. Once Périchon became ill, and for a long month I had to take care of him. But thank God I have found you, my father, and all my misfortunes are forgotten . . . . Here I am next to you to help you, to care for you, you and Pouponne."

"Or rather for see me die, my son; but it make no difference! I can only tank God who brought you back to me in time to receive my las' sigh. Listen to me good, Balthazar; when I am dead and gon' marry Pouponne as soon as you make de require preparation. Let's say inside tree mont' . . . you mus' understan' my son dat dis chil' need a protector . . . . Moreover, 'cause de ol' man be dead, dat mus' not stop de friend from have a good time . . . . I want people have fun an' eat more dan enough . . . we need enough for trow away. You understan' me?"

"Yes," replied Balthazar.

"I want everybody in de settlement invite, de ol' one, de mother, de young men, de girl, even de small chirren; all dem got to dance at de weddin' of Pouponne an' Balthazar. You understan' me, *hein*?"

"Yes," replied the couple in unison.

"An' now, my chirren, kneel down dere, bot' you, so I can bless you."

They obeyed, and *père* Landry, his two hands stretched out over the two bowed heads, in a low voice murmured a prayer for their happiness. And when Balthazar got up:

"Son," said the old man, "sometin' still boder my soul: why you don' go back to de army when you leave de ship prison? You run away to come look for us?"

"Back to the army!" repeated Balthazar with amazement, "but you haven't found out then?"

"Found out what?"

"Ah!" answered Balthazar with hesitation, "our army . . . but it no longer exists."

"How's dat? Could it have been beat?"

"No," replied the young man, "it partially melted away before the three corps of the English invasion. Pushed back on all sides by the enemy even up to Montreal, our men realized that they were only a few thousand soldiers without food or munitions . . . and it was necessary to surrender."

"And the country was lost?"

"Lost without any means of support," answered Balthazar, who dared not look at his father.

Scarcely did the young man let these words escape, than he realized that they were falling on his old father like a thunderbolt; but the question was asked in such a straightforward manner, it was by its nature difficult to avoid so that he could not have done it without lying, and a true son of Acadia does not know how to lie. The old man swayed like a tree from a great gust of wind, but he was not knocked down on the spot.

"Pouponne," he murmured while making an effort to keep himself seated on his bed, "Pouponne, come closer, my child."

The girl ran up to him; he put an arm around her neck and added in a breaking voice:

"Have you courage, my daughter?"

"Yes, father, I have been accustomed to hardship since the age of fourteen, and I am almost twenty. I will endure this last misfortune if it does not overwhelm you; if you know how to bear it with calm, with resignation."

"Can you walk long time, my chil'? Endure col' an' hunger?" asked the old man again, speaking as one speaks in a dream.

The witnesses at this scene looked at each other in consternation; certainly the old man was talking without knowing what he was saying, but the admirable girl to whom he was speaking was ready to do anything to assuage his last moments. She answered:

"You well know, *père*, that I walked here from Boston and I have seen men exhausted from fatigue drop dead on either side of me."

"It's true, my daughter! It's true! An' I love you for your bravery! Tell me: is de night all dark?"

"The storm is just now ending, but the sky is already brilliant with stars."

"Good, my chil', let's leave."

"Leave! poor *père*!" cried the girl in dismay.

"Yes. Go put aside what we gon' need for de trip; make two pack, a big one an' a lil' one . . . make de lil' one very light so it don't tire you too much . . . me, I take de big one . . . we go ahead and have Balthazar tol' to come join us . . . an' he gon' catch up 'cause his steps are longer dan ours."

"But you can't get up," observed Pouponne. "Calm yourself, I beg you . . . and tell me: where do you want to go?"

"I want go back to our own countryside . . . I want shame our boy an' call dem back under de flag of France . . . an' I want drive de English from de land dat our ancestor leave us."

"All the passable roads are closed," observed Balthazar. "The enemy has forced the inhabitants of Acadia to swear an oath of allegiance . . . your very sons have submitted to this condition."

"My sons!" cried the old man while laughing in a way that made you uneasy, "de others, maybe . . . but not my Balthazar!"

And he raised his head with all the pride, with all the nobility of a prophet done by Michelangelo.

"Balthazar like the others," said the young man; "this oath alone could open the doors of the prison for him and allow him to start looking for you, my father."

"Balthazar!" repeated *père* Landry, who seemed to have forgotten where he was; "No! Balthazar never do dat . . . dey fool you. It's not my boy, my làs' born who done dishonor himself by such a coward act! . . . by a lie! . . . He is young, he . . . he is a soldier . . . he can fight . . . an' you want me believe dat he become Englishman! . . . No! No! dose ting dere, dey are not in de blood of de Landry!"

"It was with rage in his heart that he agreed," added Balthazar, "but they left him no other way to leave prison and come to you."

"But he should have stay in prison! die dere, if he have to . . ." exclaimed the old man with a wild exaltation which resembled a state of madness. "He should have know what de English do to his family . . . . He saw his family scatter on de road of exile an' his old father, at de age of ninety all alone, strip of everything like beggar, an' have for support only dis angel whose mother was kill by de English . . . . An' him, de coward! at twenty-four, instead of fight, instead of die, he become Englishman! Ah! I say one more time, dat's not possible . . . . You lie, you who got de nerve to tell me dat my son, Balthazar Landry, dishonor himsef.

XX

Balthazar, pale as death, went to kneel at the bed of his dying father.

"*Père*," he said, "listen to me; don't condemn me before hearing me . . . if it looked like I was abandoning you, you and Pouponne, in the moment of danger, it was to obey your orders . . . . Oh! Oh! when I got back, you had left and I could do nothing for you two. It was then that I resolved to consecrate to my country the life that the English had spared me. I fought two years under the French flag, without pay and almost without food, the first in all dangers, remaining faithful to the flag of France up to the moment, when surrounded by a force ten times greater than ours, I was made prisoner and thrown into a frightful prison where I remained two years suffering tortures that only the most refined hatred could invent. After the rout of our army they opened the doors of my prison; but to let me out, they demanded the oath for which you reproach me. Foreseeing that my old father had to be somewhere, worn out by suffering and age, I told myself that it was my duty to look for him to relieve his distress. Also hoping to find the only one I loved, I swore, but with my lips only, to submit to the English, those damnable people I was getting ready to flee forever . . . . Our army no longer existed, therefore, I could not rejoin it . . . . France had abandoned her soldiers, had disowned them . . . . Was it a crime on our part to disown her in our turn, especially when it was a question of the safety of those we loved? My own country was lost . . . I couldn't do anything more for her. I believed that by giving up the two years of salary that the king of France owes me I could, without doing anything criminal, offer my work and my love to what is dearest to me after my country: my father and my fiancée! and I hoped that after finding them again, and touching the hand that I had searched for to receive its blessing, that hand would not push me away with anger and scorn . . . *Père*! Pouponne! tell me . . . am I now to be happy or cursed?"

"Happy, loved, blessed! isn't that so, my father?" cried Pouponne while putting her arm around the necks of both her fiancé and her father and bringing together in the same embrace their tear-bathed faces.

"Yes, my daughter," said the old man in a choked voice, "it is God who conquer us, my chirren, an' not de English."

After these words there was a moment of silence during which these three unfortunate people together found again the lost path of their happiness, but they were not to walk it long.

Pouponne was holding the old man in her arms when suddently she felt his whole weight on her.

"You are getting weaker, *père*," she said quite frightened, "are you worse?"

His only answer was to sink down on his bed, and they heard him murmur in a progressively weaker voice:

"My God! My God! You want it den! . . . it seem to me dat de love of France was a holy ting an' dat you didn't put it in my heart for snatch it away . . . for see it outrage . . . for me to forget it!"

He stopped for a moment completely exhausted. Then he added:

"It gon' be den," he said, "dat a strange country gon' cover my bones . . . to die at ninety . . . an' be bury far from my own people! Ah! dat's hard!"

And a tear slowly ran down the winkled cheek of the old man and fell on the hand of the girl who was holding him up. Fr. Jacques drew nearer and he took her hand silently, and although he made every effort to master his powerful emotion, it could be seen in his paleness and above all in his tear-filled eyes. He was a native son of Grand Pré; his father had been a cousin and friend of *père* Landry, and Fr. Jacques himself had always demonstrated a warm friendship for the old man whom he had followed into exile. He shuddered in spite of himself as he watched the progress of death which drew nearer. A generalized disturbance was convulsing the whole body of the dying man; his extremities were growing cold and his lips and nostrils were contracting violently. Balthazar and Pouponne, leaning over him in anguish, were following every movement of his face and watched for a salutary change and the return of his speech which seemed to have stopped forever.

"Pray with me," said the priest.

The young couple fell to their knees. Fr. Jacques continued to follow the stages of the crisis, all the while praying earnestly. After a few minutes inarticulate sounds escaped from the throat of the old man; there were jerky and incoherent phrases which soon changed into a sort of enraged delirium which showed only too well the state into which this unfortunate soul had sunk.

So incoherent had his language become, that it would be incomprehensible to anyone who had not actually been present during his death throes. This paraphrasing can only suggest the wandering of his mind and the almost visionary exaltation as death drew nearer.

"That's fine!" he shouted with a sort of rage as his finger pointed toward imaginary beings. "That's good, good Lord! it's just . . . and I thank You! Oh! you monsters it is indeed you I see: Lawrence . . . Murray . . . Winslow . . . Butler . . . . I see you in the midst of a blazing fire where devils have pushed you . . . . Look at them! oh! how the sight of their torture does me good . . . with what quivers of joy I hear their cries of agony! . . . They are asking for a drink and the demons are offering to quench their thirst with the tears of their victims. Drink, monsters! eternity will not slake your thirst! There, there are mothers, young children, old people . . . they stop you when you pass . . . all tear at your face with their fingernails, tear out your hair and in voices choked by the despair you caused cry out:

"'Give us back our children! give us back our fathers, our mothers, our fields, our churches that you looted . . . . Give us back our Acadie and our happiness.'"

He stopped short, exhausted. Pouponne gently lifted his head with one hand and with the other brought to his lips the glass containing the medication she had prepared for him. He drank not knowing what he was doing and at the end of a moment:

"Oh! listen!" he exclaimed, "listen to those heavenly songs . . . there, there, I see them, our holy women, our grandchildren, our sons, our fathers. . . . God has called them close to him to dry their tears, to fill their hearts with divine love . . . . Listen! just listen . . . they are with the angels . . . with them they are singing the hymn of deliverance . . . oh! my faithful old companion! my daughters so beautiful! so lively! . . . my sons . . . my children's children . . . . I see them all . . . there . . . they are there . . . they are calling me . . . they are waiting for me."

These last words were barely intelligible . . . a profuse and icy sweat was covering the body of the dying man; his face had assumed a calmer expression. Fr. Jacques leaned over him and said softly:

"*Père* Landry, you must die without hate; you must forgive."

"Pardon!" he cried while suddenly coming out his exhaustion as if by the effect of a powerful stimulant. In his excitement he found the strength to half-raise himself on his bed.

"Pardon the English! oh! that is impossible! Fr. Jacques! They have run my people off through the woods and over the seas . . . they have thrown them in the water to feed the fishes . . . they have interred their mortal remains in the soil of foreign countries . . . they have attempted to sell them as slaves, to close them up in the mines of Pennsylvania . . . they have forced them to take a shameful oath . . . . And when these damnable people are happy and triumphant, you want me to pardon them? No! I repeat it: never! never!"

"God wants it, my brother."

"You can be sure that God will not pardon them, he . . ."

"When He was on Calvary, he pardoned the Jews."

"Yes," replied the dying man, "but He kept an eternity of justice to punish them." "*Père* Landry," continued the priest, "think about it! I can not grant you the pardon that you refuse the others. You then want to die without receiving absolution?"

The old man, still helped by Pouponne, had raised himself to his knees as if to brace himself for the necessity of this supreme pardon imposed by religion. He had his hands joined and a wild-eyed look fixed on heaven, but little by little the words of the priest made him bow his head and shook his whole being. He started to tremble all over. And when he no longer heard the voice of Fr. Jacques, with eyes raised to heaven and in a breaking voice, he articulated these words:

"My holy wife! my children! my grandchildren! you who are all in heaven, you known through your saints' eyes if my heart is still filled with the suffering and cruelty against you. Hear me before God, the judge of all of us . . . . To have the happiness of joining you in heaven where you are waiting for me, I pardon the English for you and for me!"

"And I," said his pastor, "absolve you in the name of Our Lord Jesus Christ."

The next day when Périchon arrived accompanied by 'Tit Toine and Baptiste, *père* Landry was dead, and the pleasure of the reunion was saddened by the tears that Pouponne shed over the body of her adopted father.

XXI

Two days later one saw a funeral cortege making its way along the Mississippi in the direction of the settlement's church which was located in the middle of the cemetery. The humble coffin of undressed wood was carried by four of the most vigorous elders of Petite Cadie, and all the Acadians there walked silently behind it. Monsieur Bossier's rig was following the cortege, while in the distance you could hear the reverberating sound of the cannon. According to the custom of the Acadians, (which still exists today) one hundred and one cannon-shots were to be fired in honor of the eldest patriarch of the colony, and that patriarch was *père* Landry. Some of the young men demonstrated their sympathy and respect for the family of the deceased by complying with this practice.

The noise of the cannon caused a touching little scene that I cannot resist relating. Too old and too weak to take part in the funeral ceremony of her old friend, the Labauves' grandmother had dragged herself on to the gallery to see the burial. Hearing the cannon, she turned to her son:

"Ah! Gustin, *père* Landry die; I'm now de oldes' one aroun'. Tell de boy dey mus' not waste de powder, for dey gon' need it pretty soon to make dat cannon sing again over *mère* Labauve's coffin."

Balthazar and Pouponne were walking next to the coffin; on their pale and sad faces could be seen a calmer, softer and more resigned feeling than ordinarily seen on people stricken with such grief. Behind them were walking all the inhabitants of Petite Cadie.

The procession, after following the course of the river, entered the yard of the little church. After the prayers were said over the body of this noble martyr, after the priest had raised his voice to speak of the virtues of the one who had just left this earth, the pallbearers picked up the coffin and took it down to the new cemetery which surrounded the church and where one saw only a few wooden crosses and a grave awaiting the remains of another exile.

After some further prayers, the coffin was lowered into the grave . . . . Each one threw in a handful of soil as a final farewell and turned away in silence. Only a few people, some mothers and children, knelt before crosses that covered their loved ones.

Pouponne and Balthazar remained leaning over the edge of the grave until the gravedigger had covered up the wood of the coffin, then they got up and tearfully took the path again to the cabin, followed by Périchon who had waited for them at the gate of the cemetery.

After the death of *père* Landry, Madame Bossier herself came for Pouponne and took her to her own house.

"My dear child," she told her, "you cannot stay any longer in your father's cabin, along with these two boys, one of whom is your fiancé. At my house you will wait for the moment of your marriage, and during the three months that will go by from now to then, Balthazar will be able to make the necessary changes in the cabin and we two will take care of your trousseau. What do think about that, my dear Pouponne?"

It was with as much pleasure as gratitude that Pouponne accepted the invitation of her friend. Every day Balthazar came to visit his fiancée and was more and more astonished at the extraordinary changes he saw in her. The silly and gay peasant girl with speech and manners just a trifle common, who had never opened a book in her life, had yielded to an adorable girl of dignified and modest demeanor, correct and distinguished speech whose every movement was marked with an inimitable grace. Pouponne had matured considerably during the six years that had just gone by, and Balthazar acknowledged that she had become very pretty. Without education himself the young man, whose total book knowledge consisted of being able to read and write, could not help guessing at what treasures of knowledge the pretty little head of his fiancée contained.

Thanks to Charlotte, Pouponne had been selling her cotton articles to the New Orleans merchants and was making a substantial profit which she used almost entirely to buy books to further her education. Confronted with such an extraordinary intelligence and such a great desire to learn, Monsieur Bossier made himself the girl's teacher. Certainly, the poor child had very little time go give to study, but as soon as she had a free moment, she would run to her friends and ask them for lessons in spelling, arithmetic and geography which were soon replaced by foreign languages, history and mathematics. From the wife she would receive lessons in all types of embroidery, in which Charlotte excelled. The result of this education, though often interrupted for weeks at a time, was that at the end of four years Pouponne had passed Charlotte in all the sciences and was now making the most exquisite and charming embroidery, which at the time commanded a fabulous price.

It should be noted that our little Pouponne liked clothes; thus thanks to the money she was earning, though a good part went for the comfort of *père* Landry, she had the means to dress, without extravagance, of course, but with an elegant simplicity that Charlotte herself could not equal.

The more he knew her, the more Monsieur Bossier admitted that his pupil was a source of continual surprise for him. The taste for the beautiful seemed innate in this young creature who had never found herself before any beauty save of those nature. With nothing she would make a charming outfit, in a moment her agile fingers would transform into charming and graceful objects the crudest type of furniture. Charlotte did nothing without consulting her and my great-grandfather himself came sometime for advice or would call her when he was perplexed in his calculations and was looking for the solution. And what was most charming in this sweet child was the touching modesty that governed all her actions: instead of being proud of her learning, she would hide it and always sought to attribute it to those to whom she owed it. Her gratitude toward her friends could only be compared to the boundless marks of friendship shown in her regard.

Périchon admitted that he was afraid of his sister.

"Dat's no more our Pouponne, dat's a fine lady!" he would say.

But by means of soft entreaties she succeeded in reassuring him and making him admit that he had found again his Pouponne of the old days.

Pouponne had not failed to inform her fiancé of her intention to become schoolmistress for the village; but she encountered a formidable opposition.

"No, no," answered Balthazar, "for too long we have been separated, I won't give you up to anyone . . . you belong to me and I want you always at my side . . . . As for the children, I will see the fathers of the families and I will advise them to get together to build a big school of which Périchon will take charge. If he is not learned like you, my darling, if he does not know Latin and geography, he does know enough besides to educate the little Cajuns of the settlement. Does that suit you, dear little wife-to-be?"

Pouponne wanted everything Balthazar wanted and made no objection to his proposal.

If Madame Bossier was attached to Pouponne and treated her in all ways as an equal, Monsieur Bossier for his part felt attracted by the frank and cheerful manners of the young man; it didn't take him long to discover the intelligence, the probity, the high courage and the energy of this soul tried by so much misfortune. Fr. Jacques added more to this budding friendship by relating to my ancestor all that he knew of the past of Balthazar, and when about two months after his return, the overseer of the plantation died, Monsieur Bossier did not hesitate to offer the position to his young neighbor.

As we can imagine, Charlotte was not in the dark concerning this offer, that Balthazar accepted with the most heartfelt thanks. This position was beyond his hopes: the salary was $50.00 per month and, in addition, the overseer's house was a pretty little thing covered with crawling vines and built in Monsieur Bossier's yard, just a few steps from the main house. It was a great joy for our two friends: in the future they could see each other at any hour of the day, and even talk to each other from gallery to gallery.

Père Landry's cabin was left to Périchon, and as he was complaining that he would be too lonely there:

"Well, my boy," said Balthazar to him, "follow my example . . . get married . . . but, as for finding another Pouponne . . . it's out of the question! That's something else . . . There are not two like her from one end of the world to the other."

And the preparations for the wedding were going on: the workmen from the plantation were repairing and painting the overseer's house and under the direction of Charlotte and Pouponne were creating all sorts of furnishings for the new household. Pouponne had succeeded in putting aside a small sum which was dedicated to her trousseau. In spite of her instinctive pride, she was familiar with the customs and she knew she would offend her friends if she refused their wedding presents. Monsieur Bossier made her a present of a dozen place settings in sterling, while Charlotte decided to take charge of the bride's outfit, and Placide, having heard that the wedding was being prepared, sent the fiancée a lovely necklace of pearls that she wore the day of the ceremony.

XXII

Next to the church the Acadians had built a large house, (or rather, a shed) containing two immense rooms: one was for dancing and the other for banquets; it was there that wedding breakfasts were held. As we will recall, it had been the last wish of old Landry that the marriage of Balthazar and Pouponne be celebrated with all the magnificence possible and that all the inhabitants of Petite Cadie, men, women and children be present; he had further declared that a big dance, followed by a banquet to end all banquets should be the high point of his children's wedding. Therefore, Balthazar, in order to conform to the wishes of his father had secured the two rooms in question: in one the banquet was to be set up, in the other they would dance.

And all the Acadian women, who adored Pouponne, wanted to contribute to the wedding meal. One was sending a fat turkey, another a pair of ducks, some eggs, others still a goose, some chickens, a suckling pig, and one could see all the housewives with their hands in dough or molasses preparing cakes or enormous piles of *tac-tac* (popcorn mixed with molasses) for this dinner which was threatening to reach formidable proportions. The young men had all left to go hunting: wasn't every type of game needed for Pouponne' wedding banquet? And on the bank of the river the children and old men, line in hand, were trying to catch as many fish as possible.

Pouponne had neither mother nor sisters who could take charge of the preparations for her marriage: therefore, she sent for Zozo and Titine Labauve and put everything in their hands. Those two took on about a dozen friends as helpers and things gave every promise of working like clockwork. The day before the wedding one could see leaving the Bossier plantation a large farm wagon filled with provisions of all sorts and on which rode five cooks and a dozen helpers; it was headed toward the banquet hall where Zozo and Titine were giving orders like queens.

"I want to go to your wedding-party, my dear," Charlotte had said to her friend."

"No, no," replied the latter, "It's not your place, Charlotte. Come to the church; I want you to be a witness to my happiness, but a Cajun wedding celebration is not made for you; you would make the guests feel uneasy . . . they could make you blush. I, myself . . . I feel it is wrong to say it for I am showing my pride. This will be the first and last Cajun wedding celebration that I will attend. The vulgarity appalls me, but Balthazar and I wanted to conform in every way to the desires of *père* Landry and we will have, I am afraid, a real cannibal wedding feast."

The day the marriage was to take place Fr. Jacques sent his rig early to pick up the couple. Charlotte had wanted to take Pouponne in her carriage, but it was against the rules, the couple was supposed to ride together at the head of the bridal procession. Charlotte had to be satisfied with following the rig with her husband, both all alone in their fine carriage.

Fr. Jacques' *calèche* was the only one in this Acadian village. For those who have never seen this type of vehicle, I must say that it was simply a sort of buggy without any top and made entirely of wood: frame, wheels and all. The Acadians of every period had clung to the *calèche* and even today one finds it among the rich as well as among the poor. But, as the inhabitants of Petite Cadie had no money for a *calèche*, and as everybody wanted to go to the celebration and as the church was quite far away, they had to get there the best way possible. For the men it was nothing, but the women! ah! you should have seen them passing along the river, barefoot, through the midst of the mud, all loaded down with packages containing their footwear and dance dresses. Most of them had their heads covered with papillotes, that you could see beneath the handkerchief that they had thrown over their hair and tied under their chins.

But the most curiously entertaining part of the procession for the bystanders was the men on horseback and the women clambered up behind them. Often on the same mount one saw an Acadian with his wife, or sister, or fiancée behind him . . . plus one or two children. At intervals one could see a poor little creole horse bending under the weight of a half-dozen children mounted bareback. Like the women on foot, those on horseback were barefoot and were carrying their dance clothes in a package, but they fixed it over the horse's rump.

As I have said, the church was far away, and an early start was necessary if the revelers were to have time to enjoy themselves. Accordingly, at seven o'clock this whole group of people was on the way. Ahead you could see the couple's *calèche* driven by Balthazar while Pouponne was trying her best to keep her veil and crown away from the umbrella she was holding in the other hand. Right behind them came the carriage of Monsieur Bossier and finally all those on horseback and on foot.

Pouponne was right when she told Charlotte that she did not have the faintest idea what an Acadian wedding celebration was; she was destined to learn and at some personal cost.

Scarcely had the procession gone a half-mile and picked up all those remaining on the roadside, when a formidable outcry was heard and all the men, bottle in hand, came up, and every mouth cried at the same time:

"Hurrah for Pouponne! Hurrah for Balthazar! To de healt' of Pouponne! To de healt' of Balthazar!"

And at each "hurrah! the friends of the couple downed a mouthful of brandy from the bottles which had just appeared.

"Good Lord!" exclaimed my great-grandfather while his wife was holding her hands over her ears, "those people will be completely drunk before we are halfway there."

They did arrive at the church and the couple, followed by Monsieur Bossier, his wife and all the men in the procession entered it silently. But where were the women? Upon arriving they had all, shoes in hand, run to the river's edge they had to clean themselves before putting on their shoes; and when all these feminine feet were quite clean, they put on shoes and stockings and made their way to the banquet hall, which had been changed for the moment into a dressing room. There the packages had been left; there they took out the papillotes and put on their skirts and and many-hued bodices while exchanging a fair number of double-entendre remarks. And while all this was going on, the priest was waiting at the altar and the couple kneeling in the first pew were praying while waiting the good pleasure of Mesdames Théogène, Théodule, Télesphore, Sosthène, Térence, Onésiphore, etc. and of Mesdemoiselles Manette, 'Tite Mine, Tonton, Arthémise, Modeste and others.

Finally they entered without sparing the hubbub and when they settled the best they could, the priest made a sign to the couple to come closer. As Pouponne was getting up, Monsieur Bossier advanced and offered his arm. By leading the girl to the altar, my ancestor demonstrated his friendship and respect for her. On seeing Pouponne on the arm of this important gentleman the women did not hesitate to raise a murmur of surprise and admiration.

The ceremony was short: the pastor knew it was unnecessary to talk of love and fidelity to this young couple tried by so much misfortune.

XXIII

There was a rather amusing little scene after the ceremony. The law demands three witnesses for any marriage, and after presenting the register to the couple and, after seeing them sign it, Fr. Jacques asked if there were in the church three persons of the masculine sex who knew how to write and would be willing to serve as witnesses. Monsieur Bossier and Périchon presented themselves; but alas! not a single individual in this whole crowd could sign his name and the priest felt he would be obliged to be satisfied with two witnesses, when 'Tit Toine, dressed in his altar boy's cassock, tugged at the sleeve of Fr. Jacques' surplice while saying:

"Father, I know sign my name, you teach me yousef . . . can I not do like de men de day of de weddin' of my sister an' put my *pataraffe* (initials) on the register like Périchon an' de big *missié*?"

"Of course," replied Fr. Jacques smiling at his altar boy, "put your name there next to Périchon's. That's fine . . . and thank heaven, I have my three witnesses."

After all this was done, Pouponne saw herself surrounded by the women who in their somewhat vigorous demonstrations of affection almost smothered her. She had to kiss everybody, and everybody had to kiss her; then, as 'Tit Toine used to say, everybody started to kiss his neighbor, and this exchange of kisses lasted almost an hour. Charlotte, seeing all that and fearing that the kisses would eventually reach her, took French leave, satisfying herself for the moment with a waved farewell to her friend.

As soon as the embracing was finished, the joyous group headed toward the dance hall, but before getting there, they brought out the brandy bottles and this time their cry was:

"Hurrah! for Madame Balthazar!" which made a formidable echo.

This cry repeated by two hundred voices only stopped at the moment when the wedding procession was entering the dance hall. It was ten o'clock and the meal was to be served at precisely noon; then as soon as it was finished, they would start dancing again, and the dancing would last through the daylight hours. Such was the program which had been announced by Zozo. It was to her and to her sister-in-law Titine that Pouponne had entrusted the supervision of the banquet and the wedding dance, and they discharged their duty wonderfully, especially Titine, who, having married twice, knew from experience what an Acadian wedding celebration was like.

All around the dance hall they had improvised benches by putting planks on tree trunks carried in for the occasion. The orchestra was composed, first of all, of the settlement's violin player, the handsome Etienne Aucoin, who on this memorable day had taken on as helpers three of Monsieur Bossier's Negroes, who were considered first-class musicians. They were all standing up, each on a different barrel, and the orchestra leader, Etienne, the violin player, all the while waving his bow, was beating time with his foot and head at the same time. One of the Negroes also played the violin: as for the two others, one was holding a triangle which he was hitting with an iron rod, while the other was shaking a fistful of bones and making the most grotesque contortions. The room was to be lighted later by tallow candles made by the women. The candles were pushed into holes in a little plank that was nailed to the wall.

You don't dance without refreshment, so Zozo and Titine in their tender solicitude for the guests, had decorated the room with all the refreshments they had at their disposal. On the chimney was a triple row of brandy bottles accompanied by two little tin cups.

"You got pick out lil' one," Titine had said, "dat will keep dem from get drunk."

Poor woman! she realized a little too late that finding the cups too small, the drinkers were not in the least embarrassed to fill them several times in a row.

In each corner of the room was a barrel: the first was filled with sweet potatoes cooked in the oven, the second with peanuts, and the third with those big wild nuts found in the woods and which the pigs like so much. As for the fourth, it was full of water, and a long-handled dipper was hanging from it at the end of a string attached by a nail. In addition to these refeshments, two or three little boys were passing back and forth among the dancers, stopping before the benches where the mothers and old maids sat, some carrying a large coffee pot full of delicious coffee and the others an enormous cup destined to receive it. They would go from one to the other, presenting the coffee and cup to the guests while repeating each time:

"Dis coffee, he sweet; Zozo herself, she put de suga' in it."

Pouponne could hardly believe her eyes: now used to the refinements of proper society, she felt revolted by so much vulgarity. To conform to custom she got in place with Balthazar, but after the first dance, she refused all the partners, who presented themselves, saying she was overwhelmed by a terrible headache. The young men did not like this excuse, and they went away saying:

"She lie . . . she got nottin' wrong wit' her but pride dat she pick up from de people at de big house . . . . She tink she too big to dance wit' poor boy like us."

At precisely noon, two little boys opened the door between the two rooms and shouted at the top of their lungs:

"Dinner, everybody! Dinner is serve in dere!"

And by two's they made their way to the banquet hall without too much commotion. It was indeed a real Rabelaisian, if not cannibal feast. To make the gumbo they had used a sugar cauldron and had put in five turkeys and at least three or four dozen chickens. It was by the scores that you counted the tom turkeys and the suckling pigs; two sheep and two deer could be seen, not to mention the fowl, the game, the fish, and all sorts of good things. All the regional specialties were there: *machou* (grains of green corn cooked in boiling grease), jambalaya, beans and rice and even *couche couche* (corn meal mixed with water and cooked in boiling grease) were spread among the finest games, cakes, jams, creams, pumpkin pies, and mountains of *tac-tac*. Monsieur Bossier, in addition to the succulent provisions, had sent a hundred bottles of wine which were spread out on the table. This table had accommodations for a hundred and fifty guests, but according to the tradition, the ladies sat down first and were served by the men. Each guest had been told to bring his plate and knife; the plates had been sent in advance. Scarcely seated, each guest pulled a knife from his pocket, and that one utensil sufficed; only the newlyweds had a complete place setting. As for glasses, in many places they were replaced by tin cups or dippers.

The beginning of the meal passed rather quickly; the presence of women made itself felt, but when the hungriest were satisfied, the songs began and as the old friends of Balthazar remembered his voice, one of them shouted:

"De groom! de groom! we got have de groom give us a lil' song."

Balthazar, who had promised himself to go along with all the demands of his guests, got up with a smile and a glass of wine in his hand and began an old favorite of the local men:

Love is a good fo' nottin' dog
Dat do more bad dan good.
Men on prison ship
Don't complain 'bout rowin'
You trouble, dat's sugar
Next to de trouble of lovin'.

It was on a spring day
Dat I call mysef in love,
De lover of a brunette
Beautiful like a Cupid
Her hair all fix up
Light on her head like butterfly.

And at each verse the crowd shouted, the guests struck their glasses with their knives and made a thousand grimaces and as many contortions from which Pouponne turned her eyes in disgust. Balthazar, who had stopped for a moment, resumed:

She got two shinin' eye
Like diamond
An' de scarlet
On de coat of de English
Look like yellow
Next to her fresh skin.

She got plenty life
Jus' like bachelor of t'irty!
How she go t'rough de work!
Well! you got see it!
De devil take me! no queen
Don't wash an' bleach dat good.

An' dat ting pretty like flower
Belong to me by mysef.
An' now dat de pries'
'As tie us together
She is today my lil' wife
An' I'm her good servant.

Drink boys; sing girls!
Hurrah for de married people!
An' specially . . . I'm only tell you dis:
Do quick like me!
De pries' is dere . . . all ready for make
De number one from de number two!

XXIV

It is impossible to describe the excitement that followed this song; there was noise enough to drive a person crazy . . . and poor Pouponne, who didn't have the courage to taste anything, felt a frightful migraine coming over her more and more.

Although the men were not at the table, they found the means to have passed to them by their wives or sweethearts, not only food, but bottles of wine. As a result, heads began to get hot; trivial remarks and some with double-entendre were addressed directly to the bride, whose face turned a deep red. To stop this talk and noise, Zozo had the idea to call to her aid the handsome violin player, who, because he played the violin and knew how to sing, put on airs (according to what Térencine said) and passed for the most elegant in the settlement.

"Etienne! Etienne Aucoin! a song," cried Zozo.

And all the women with a single voice repeated:

"Yes, Etienne, a song."

And the handsome Etienne, making a few objections to enhance his performance and quite proud deep down inside, got up on the bench and after bowing first to the bride and then to the rest of the company began his song. At the end of each verse the singer would stop and with most comical gestures speak the end of the verse he had started by singing. Let's listen to the song of our violin player. When he would reach the refrain, all the men and even some women (Térencine among them) would repeat it with him. I will let you imagine for yourself the ensuing din:

One day on de port wit' Manon
I was talk to her sweet 'bout love
An' easy dat can be believe.
A fancy dresser man came by us
An' want make sweet eye.

Spoken: *Sapristi*! Am I jealous! To want take away my woman; dat's like to want lick my butter and take me for fool.

Refrain:

I want be dog
Who wit' kick an' punch
Bus' for him de ugly face an' jaw.
De watchman who was dere
Come over for stop de fight
An' easy dat can be believe.
Jus' for tell him to go 'way
Didn't he want to shoot me?

Spoken: Me 'cause I'm good Cajun, I spit on you gunpowder an' give it back to you good for nottin' an' whass mo':

I want be dog . . .

My sweet one an' me we leave
Look for mushroom.
An' easy dat can be believe.
A no-good buggy dat was pass by
Splash mud on bot' de two of us.

Spoken: "I who was wit' dry clothes, who like be clean an' don't want people dirty my clothes, got reason to say:"

I want be dog . . .

Dat mess up our white stocking
An' make us look like some tramp
An' easy dat can be believe.
One lil' young man who see us
An' wanting to mock us, was laughing.

Spoken: "Tell me den, *missié* angel, you run 'way from heaven to make fun of people?"

I want be dog . . .

Since we people dance in de garden,
We gon' dance our lil' dance

An' easy dat can be believe.
De damn violin player who out-of-tune
Wanted ask me for some peanut.

Spoken: "Some . . . Wait, mister out-of-tune, I'm gon' get some money for buy yousef a bandage dat do more good."

I want be dog . . .

At end of day wit' no one to see
I take Manon into a lil' corner;
An' easy dat can be believe.
I tell her, mamzelle, you got
Give me lil' kiss, or else.

Spoken: "For respect dat I owe you, good behave girl, believe me, mamzelle, one lil' kiss, he is sweetness, it is true! No, no mamzelle don't back away, 'cause . . . I only tell you dis:"

I want be dog . . .

I cannot describe the enthusiasm and the burst of laughter with which the song was received, at each of Etienne's contortions the hands clapped and, as I said, the refrain was repeated in a chorus by more than a hundred voices. Taking advantage of tumult, Pouponne begged Balthazar to take her into the dance hall.

"I am suffocating in here," she said.

Since the departure of Placide, we have lost sight of the sweet 'Tite Mine. What had happened to her? A new Ariadne, was she still weeping over the abandonment of a new Theseus? Had she died of grief after Placide left her? To answer these two questions we are going to follow the newlyweds into the dance hall where several couples had preceded them, and there in a corner we will find again Térencine's daughter prettier and more coquettish than ever, seated next to Périchon who is looking at her with admiring eyes wide open. But what are they doing so close to each other? What is provoking their merriment? Ah! I see: 'Tite Mine's little muslin apron is filled with peanuts that Périchon is shelling with the greatest dexterity and which they are munching in the midst of their outbursts of laughter. One can say a lot of things while eating peanuts, and certainly what the brother of Pouponne said chased far from this charming head the memory of Placide as she bestowed her most charming smiles on him.

Upon seeing the newlyweds leave, the women get up and yield the tables to the men; the black musicians are recalled and the dance resumes in full swing. But look: the first in place are 'Tite Mine and Périchon.

XXV

Night has come, the candles are lit, and the dinner keeps going on. One hour, two hours pass, and soon a frightful tumult is heard in the banquet hall. People are quarreling, fighting, and throwing pieces of poultry and bottles at each other. With the cries of the combatants are mixed threats and horrible cursing. The wives who stayed in the banquet hall are weeping and trying to lead their husbands away . . . they get nothing but insults and blows for their trouble . . . . And in the other room people are dancing and having a good time.

Zozo's Gustin is among the fighters; seeing that she cannot snatch him from the hands of those who are holding him, the poor woman in tears runs to get Fr. Jacques. The priest has seen too many Acadian celebrations not to be familiar with the results . . . he seeks to calm the din, but he is dealing with drunk and raving men who do not want to listen to him.

While passing by a group slightly less intoxicated, but just as dangerous as the first, the pastor hears words which make him blush with indignation. It is Etienne Aucoin who is talking and describing to his comrades a plan that they heartily approve and which stirs up their laughter and cries of approbation. It is to get hold of Balthazar and force him to get drunk, no less.

"Even if we got trow whiskey down de troat," adds the good violin player, "an' after dat we lock him up 'til tomorrow . . . It's me who gon' take charge of dis lil' man. An' den, like dat, dat pretty Pouponne who like to turn her nose up on poor folk, who is proud like one sun . . . who tink she too big for dance wit' us, she gon' have go back by hersef in de *calèche* of de pries'. Ah! Ah! dat's a good trick! right, ma frens?"

But he had not taken into account his host, or rather Fr. Jacques. The latter, seeing himself unable to calm these wild men who were fighting on top the tables, ordered the women to put out the candles and hurried to warn the newlyweds about the plot being hatched against them.

"Come with me to the priest's house; my *calèche* is ready. You can leave at once and when those wretches come looking for you, you will already be far away."

Pouponne and Balthazar hastened to obey and warmly thanked Fr. Jacques. And while on one side people were dancing with all the impulse of youth and while our couple was fleeing, the battle in the banquet hall continued unabated in spite of the darkness. The combatants had succeeded in getting off the tables and now were rolling on the floor in the midst of roast turkeys, gravies, hams and bottles. We must imagine what a deplorable condition they were in when they reappeared on the dance floor. Their evening party lasted until dawn. At the moment when the sun was coming up in all its splendor, the procession formed anew; each rider picked up his mate again. They had to go looking for the children whom they found asleep in every corner. Those who had come on foot also started out. But how everything was so changed in the appearance of this group! Without counting the black eyes, the smashed noses, more than one headdress had been lost, more than one bodice and skirt dirtied or torn, and the most profound silence replaced the cries of joy of the day before. Each was going home and passed in front of the house of Périchon, who on reaching his cabin, found himself last in the procession, the Labauves having remained a few hours to put some order back into this terrible disorder.

When Périchon found himself alone:

"Ah! let's hope it won't be for long!" he said with a sigh while thinking about the sweet 'Tite Mine.

Pouponne could now say that she had seen an Acadian wedding, but it made her sick for three days, while Charlotte laughed to the point of tears listening to Balthazar's version of the wedding celebration of Pouponne and Balthazar.

Upon leaving the priest's house, the couple had gone directly home and had taken possession of the overseer's cottage. Every day Monsieur Bossier patted himself on the back just a little more for having turned over the running of his plantation to Balthazar Landry. As for the two women, they could not help but thank the fate that had brought them together.

"It is to you, Charlotte," Pouponne would say, "that I owe the little that I am worth."

"But," Charlotte would reply, "is it not you, Pouponne, who brought me to know the supreme happiness of doing good! is it not you who taught me those sweet virtures which make you so beloved by all near you?"

The children of the two families grew up together, and twenty years after the marriage of Pouponne and Balthazar, another marriage took place on the

Bossier plantation: that of the attractive Marie Bossier, fifth daughter of Charlotte, with Louis, the eldest son of Judge Balthazar Landry. We might add that at this moment our Balthazar was not only judge, but also one of the richest people in Saint James Parish.

When the American Revolution broke out, the hatred of the young Acadian against the English was rekindled suddenly and he rushed to the aid of his adopted country. Monsieur Bossier was not destined to remain behind; scarcely did he learn of the arrival of Lafayette in America, than he enlisted under the general's flag. Like Balthazar, he distinguished himself in the army, but less fortunate than his young overseer, he was seriously wounded and remained half-blind for many years. It is there that the devotion of Charlotte showed itself in all its sublimity! and thanks to her care and prayers, God permitted the one she loved so much to recover his sight and health.

XXVI

Before ending this story, we are going back to pick up our young friend Placide, who at the time of the marriage of his niece and of the son of Pouponne, was one of the richest and most esteemed citizens of Bossier Parish, which as a sign of esteem, his fellow citizens had named after him. [Editor's note: As previously noted, this is not historical.]

After his escapade with 'Tite Mine, Placide stayed two years in college; he graduated with highest honors, and his brother called him home. But not for long, for the young man was soon to return to New Orleans to study law with one of the leading jurists of the capital.

Placide, during his college days, often wrote to his sister-in-law, but he never spoke of 'Tite Mine in his letters, and Charlotte imitated his silence; thus, he was completely ignorant of what had become of his old sweetheart. He arrived and still the name of 'Tite Mine was not pronounced. Certainly, Placide had not forgotten the little Acadian girl; she had been undoubtedly the prettiest girl in the settlement; she danced well, and our young Fleming had found great pleasure in being around her; he would laugh while noting the jealousy of the Acadians, and whatever he may have said, he had assured her many a time that he adored her.

But today he blushed at this indiscretion and the unpleasantness to which it had exposed his brother. Deep down inside he felt a secret grudge against 'Tite Mine and blamed her for all the insults of Térencine. That's why they never talked about her and did not want others to talk about her. But he had not counted on his host or on Charlotte. The young woman, having fun at his expense, had her heart set on teaching him a lesson.

The day after he returned to the plantation, Charlotte asked him to run a little errand to Périchon's: it concerned a collection of books that Monsieur Bossier had sent from the city for the young teacher.

It was about four in the afternoon when our young man lightheartedly set out, the package of books under his arm. Approaching the cabin, he stopped to listen to a youthful woman's voice repeating the refrain of an Acadian song he recalled having heard sung by 'Tite Mine.

The song, whose last words the singer was repeating at the moment of Placide's arrival, went like this:

When I was young an' pretty,
I had one beau
Fill wit' life an' hot like burning coal,
Young, handsome an' strong!
I see de spark
Shine in his eye . . .
For a tramp
De good-for-nottin' leave me dere.

Every week he put on a clean white shirt
Two time.
An' look like captain
Wit' a silver watch an'
Fine scarlet stocking
Always curl by my hand
Like a poodle dog.

At night whan I sleep
I tink about my *coquin*,
But de pleasure wake me
Holding' my pillow . . .
Luck is gon' an' change,
An' now his new sweetheart
Chew on de sugar-almond
An' me on de bitter gall.

Wit' de tear I cry
I fill a bucket.
I'm all by mysef . . .
An' dat's my secret.

De pas' is but a dream,

No sense; one nottin'
But I sponge it out my mind,
If he comes back to me.

Before the last words Placide, who had recognized the voice, felt himself strangely moved. His heart was beating at the memory of this child whom he reproached himself for leaving in so cowardly a way.

"Her despair must have been terrible! she loved me so much! poor 'Tite Mine! but what is she doing here in Périchon's cottage? . . . no doubt taking lessons."

He knocked, and a voice from the inside answered:

"Push de door; it's not close."

He entered . . . and, as he expected, found himself in the presence of 'Tite Mine. Like the young Acadian girl Madame Bossier had seen on the gallery at Térencine's five years earlier, 'Tite Mine had opened her blouse and on her firm, white breast an infant was clinging. A double cry came out at the same time:

"'Tite Mine!"

"*Missié* Placide!"

"Mon Dieu! from where you come like dat, *Missié* Placide? As true as I am one decent woman, I tink you dead an' you look to me like one ghost!" cried the young woman in a stream of language while in her amazement forgetting to cover her bosom.

"And no doubt that is why you married somebody else," said Placide in a voice with a little tone of bitterness in it.

"Come on!" she said while shrugging her shoulders and continuing to rock her child who remained clinging to her breast, "if it's for tell me some joke like dat you come *Missié* Placide, it's better for you go away . . . for I tell you one ting, good time an' fool around' are all over for me."

The young man was looking at her and wondering while seeing her half-dressed in front of him how he could have loved such an uncouth creature. However, he continued:

"I really loved you, 'Tite Mine!"

"I don't say no . . . maybe so, but you know good an' well, *Missié* Placide, dat never, no time you have idea for take me for your *légitime*."

"Didn't I tell you a hundred times that I loved you, 'Tite Mine?"

"An' maybe two hundred time, too . . . but what dat prove? Dere are some boy who got so much love in dere heart dat dey yell it from roof top an' find a way to share dem sef wit' all de girl dey see . . . like butterfly dat make politeness to one flower an' den go compare it to another. An' worse shame still on dem dat sweet talk de girl, dat act like parrot dat talk, but dey talk wit' out know demsef what dey say. But wait, *Missié* Placide, less talk 'bout sometin' else . . . . you got a lot of sweet tings in your private garden dese days?"

"'Tite Mine," continued the young man, "you behaved shamefully toward me. Why did you send Térencine to my brother's house with all sorts of complaints against me?"

"Me send my mama somewhere? Never! dere you go say fool ting again . . . Yes, it's your brother, who 'cause we dance few time at de big dance, 'cause I done accept your 'tention an' your present jus' to be polite (an' all good girl can do dat), he call me trashy girl, boy-chaser . . . say he gon' hang me an' make my mama be whip wit' some branch, an' dat by one big black man."

As we can see, Térencine not only did not hold her tongue, but used it to curse and even more frequently to lie.

"All that is false, 'Tite Mine, but you are right, the time of flings is passed for us. Who is your husband?"

"What, you don' know?"

"Of course not . . . I didn't even know you were marrried."

"I'm de wife of Périchon Thériot, de broder of Pouponne," said 'Tite Mine with a sort of pride that did not escape Placide; "an'," she continued, "he de mos' good an' de most' nice boy on dis eart'."

All of a sudden she got up and pointing to the pack of books that the young man had been holding under his arm:

"It's him you want to see, right, an' me I was pass time like talk over de fence."

She went to the window and in a strong voice called:

"Périchon! Périchon!"

"What's the matter with that woman? here I am," said a voice from the outside.

"He dig in our garden when he finish school . . . . Ah! *Missié* Placide," added the young woman with tears in her eyes, "it's one good husband dat de *Bon Dieu* give me dere . . . an' I love him! ah! so much! so much!"

At that moment the young school master was coming in and Placide hastened to complete his errand by turning over to him the pack of books. He did not stay long in spite of Périchon's invitation to have a glass of wine with him.

Upon leaving he extended his hand to the young man and bowed to his old girlfriend:

"Adieu, Madame Périchon," he said.

"*Adjeu, Missié* Placide," she replied and gave her finest curtsy.